PUFF

The Roman in Your Garden

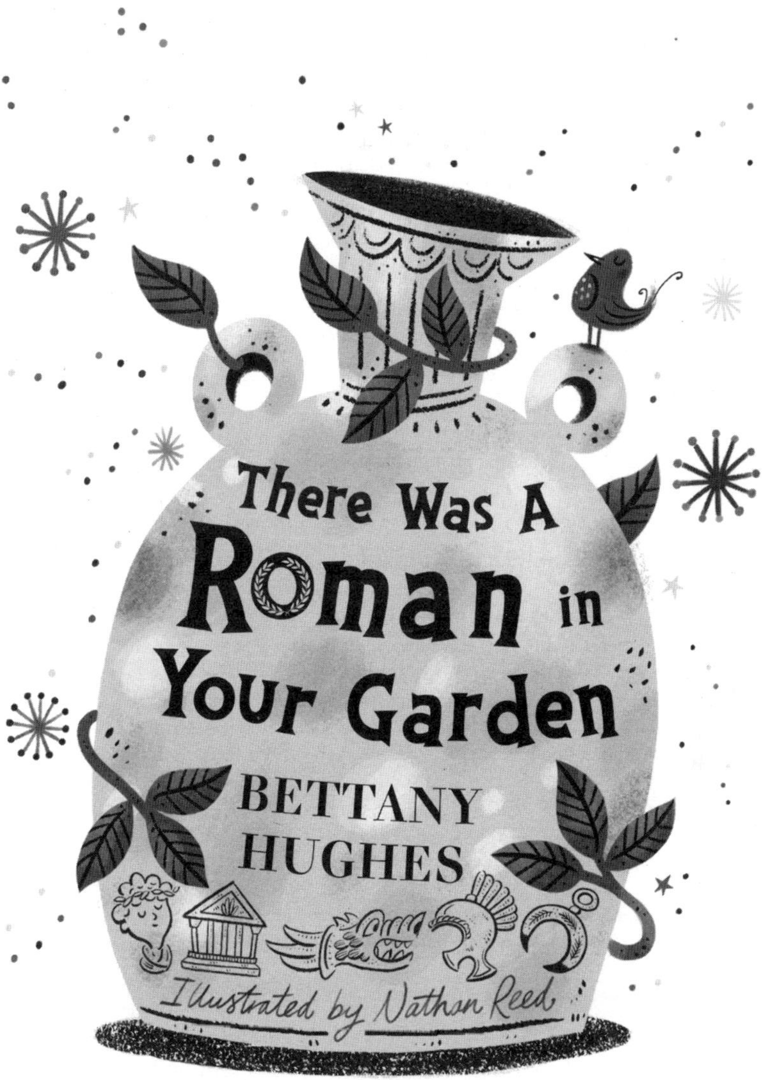

There Was A Roman in Your Garden

BETTANY HUGHES

Illustrated by Nathan Reed

PUFFIN BOOKS

UK | USA | Canada | Ireland | Australia
India | New Zealand | South Africa

Puffin Books is part of the Penguin Random House group of companies
whose addresses can be found at global.penguinrandomhouse.com

www.penguin.co.uk
www.puffin.co.uk
www.ladybird.co.uk

First published 2025

001

Text copyright © Bettany Hughes, 2025
Illustrations © Nathan Reed, 2025

The moral right of the author/illustrator has been asserted
No part of this book may be used or reproduced in any manner for the
purpose of training artificial intelligence technologies or systems.
In accordance with Article 4(3) of the DSM Directive 2019/790,
Penguin Random House expressly reserves this work from the
text and data mining exception.

Text design by Mandy Norman
Printed in Great Britain by Clays Ltd, Elcograf S.p.A.

The authorized representative in the EEA is Penguin Random House Ireland,
Morrison Chambers, 32 Nassau Street, Dublin D02 YH68

A CIP catalogue record for this book is available from the British Library

ISBN: 978-0-241-662151-1

All correspondence to:
Puffin Books
Penguin Random House Children's
One Embassy Gardens, 8 Viaduct Gardens, London SW11 7BW

Penguin Random House is committed to a
sustainable future for our business, our readers
and our planet. This book is made from Forest
Stewardship Council® certified paper.

For my delightful godchildren.
Thank you so much for being wonderful, I'm very
proud of you – Laura, Daisy, Freya, Charlie and Mercy.
And with thanks to top readers Arlo and Evie!

Contents

The Mysterious Treasure Chest . . .	1
The *Bulla*	13
The *Lunula*	25
The World's First Pizza	35
The Mystery Instrument	41
The Incense-Burner	47
The Nit Comb	57
The Perfume Bottle	63
The Crib	71
Knucklebones	77
More Toys!	85
Pens and Writing Tablets	95
Shoes	109
Slave Tags	115
Mummy Portraits	121

Crocodile Armour	133
The Dragon Standard	143
The Map	149
Garnets and Jewels	161
Horse Jewellery	171
Paw-Printed Roof Tiles	181
What an Adventure!	191
The Hall of Fame	197
Acknowledgements	215

Hi there! My name is Bettany Hughes. I'm a historian, and for my job, I get to travel across the world uncovering the truth about the past. But this particular voyage of discovery is going to be closer to home... and very exciting!

Isn't it great when you find something you thought you'd lost? It could be your favourite jumper that had buried itself in the back of your wardrobe. Or an old toy that fell under your bed. Finding it is like discovering an unexpected present from the past, isn't it?! Well, in this book, we'll be re-finding very cool things from a very long time ago.

People in ancient times – and I'm talking between 1,500 and 2,500 years ago – lost things all the time. This was probably because they were often bumping around on horses, donkeys and mules, so stuff would jiggle out of their bags, their saddle packs or off the back of their carts. Or it could also be because they were allowed to drop their rubbish on the street and down old wells. Sometimes, sadly, it was because they left things behind in their cities or towns when they were running away from unexpected dangers, like the fires that often tore through ancient settlements. Who knows what precious treasures have been lost forever...

To try to stop this, people sometimes chose to seal their treasure up in sacks, boxes and even old wine jars. They would hide these stashes of treasure underground, or in caves or tombs (large vaults used to bury the dead), or along riverbanks, maybe even deep in desert sands. Ancient people did this to keep their most precious and beloved items safe and sound, away from prying eyes and prying hands. These treasure-buriers might have planned to come back to get their possessions one day, but sometimes this just wasn't possible: perhaps their lands were being taken over by invaders, or they forgot the exact location of their hiding place, or even something really dramatic happened to them, like being kidnapped by pirates (that happened a lot in ancient times!). Or perhaps they simply died before they could return to dig up their carefully concealed belongings.

When people's possessions got left behind like this, the treasure would lie lost and forgotten for decades, centuries or even millennia (that's the word for 'thousands of years'). These lost treasures are called 'hoards' – and these hoards can turn up all over the place. I've found lots of hoards, some buried thousands of years ago, in fields, cities, hillsides, even at the bottom of the sea. Sometimes these hoards appear in pretty unexpected places – like under park benches or in ordinary back gardens! Hoards are packed with clues

and tell us so much brilliant information about life in the past.

I think we should explore a truly fascinating treasure hoard together. Come with me, will you? Let's imagine you've gone out into your garden one day and spotted something you've not seen before sticking out of the ground, something glinting in the sunshine. You see a pattern on the side of what looks like a wooden box. Those patterns look Roman to me. Let's dig it up together to find out what's inside!

It *really is* an ancient Roman chest, which means . . . there must have once been a Roman in **YOUR** garden! Imagine that. Around 2,000 years ago, a Roman was walking this very ground where your back garden now is, digging up the earth and burying some of their most prized possessions.

They've left us a hoard. And this is no ordinary hoard...

it's a **massive, full-to-bursting TREASURE CHEST!**

It's basically a Roman time capsule.
So, are you up for investigating it?
You are? **Fantastic!**

TAH DAH!
Here it is!

This particular mysterious treasure chest is extra special because it was packed up and buried by a Roman child in ancient times.

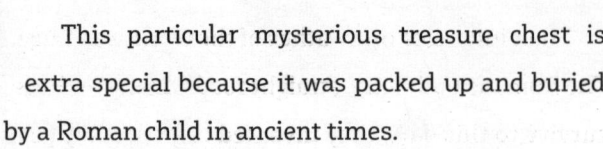

So, who were the Ancient Romans?

The ancient Roman period was an incredibly exciting time in history. Starting in Rome around 500 BCE, the Romans would create one of the most powerful and influential empires the world has ever seen. By 117 CE, Rome ruled one fifth of the world's population and had land that stretched all the way from Europe into parts of Asia and north Africa.

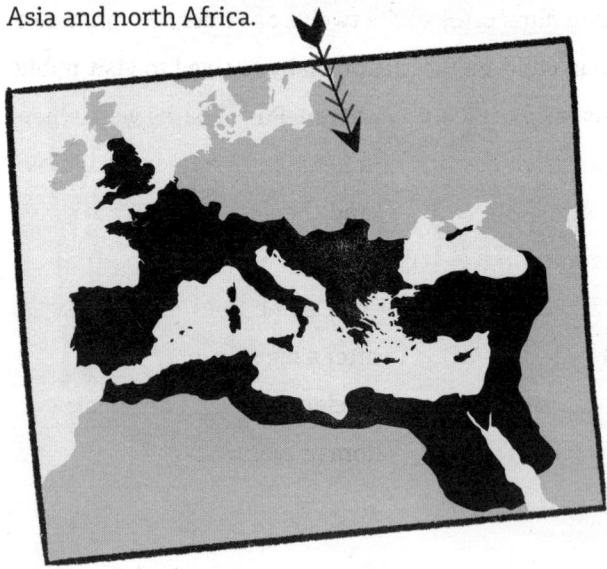

Their influence on swathes of the world was huge. The Romans built long, straight roads (many of these survive to this day); they invented cement; they gave us our calendar, with its 365 days and a leap year every four years; they had fast-food stalls just like we do – and yes, they loved pizza (they might even have invented it!). So, when we learn about the Romans, we learn a whole lot about ourselves, too.

Unpacking this treasure chest will also show us what it was like to be a young person 2,000 years ago. Like you, children were given toys to play with, some learned to read and write, and there were certain places children couldn't go to and things they couldn't do until they were older (just like you're not supposed to watch certain films until you're twelve or fifteen). For instance, Roman children weren't officially allowed to visit public baths until they were eighteen. Public baths were where adults used to go to sit in hot steam, get scrubbed down and massaged with oil, and then plunge into cold mini swimming pools. (These pools were a bit like those freezing cold ice baths you sometimes see football or rugby players sitting in after a big match!)

Some experiences in ancient Rome can seem familiar, but in many ways the Roman world was very different to life as we know it today. A truly horrible thing was that there were huge numbers of enslaved people living in the empire. These enslaved men, women and children – many millions of them – were usually just ordinary people whose homelands had been taken over by the Romans, or who had been captured in battle or traded in slave markets.

Children born into an enslaved family had no freedom whatsoever; enslaved people had no rights and were forced to work for no payment. Roman slaves had to do all kinds of work – from being teachers, to labouring as farmers, to mending shoes or cleaning out those public baths I was just talking about. There was not a single town or farm across the Roman world, from Rome's meteoric rise around 2,300 years ago, to its fall in the fifth century CE, that did not have enslaved people slaving away in it.

The ancient Romans also had different religions to those

we see today. They worshipped Roman gods, goddesses and mythical heroes, including Mars (the god of war, whom the planet Mars is named after), Venus (the goddess of love, and also the name of a planet), and Hercules, a megastrong ancient Greek superhero.

The Romans really believed these beings were real, and that they travelled through the world either helping people in trouble or, more often than not, creating mischief for them! For instance, they believed that the gods and goddesses would do things like force you to fall in love with someone who was already married or encourage people to lie to others in order to get them into trouble.

Outrageous!

Roman gods were also believed to whip up giant storms, earthquakes and floods to punish people they were cross with. Gods and goddesses were definitely not to be messed with!

Something we *do* have in common is that, like us, the Romans had hospitals. They regularly used clever natural medicines, although back then, many diseases and conditions couldn't be treated. For instance, a simple splinter could get infected and easily become fatal. People could also come down with a nasty cold or be bitten by a spider or a snake and die as a result. Not surprisingly, then, people often died very young.

So now you know a litte bit more about who the Romans were, I think it's time to lift the lid off the treasure chest, don't you? Carefully now... remember, it hasn't been opened for 2,000 years. Let's take a look inside and discover the chest's secrets, so we can see what life was like for children thousands of years ago.

Children just like
YOU.

Let's start with that smooth, gleaming, shiny object. Can you see it? Pick it up and you'll feel the metallic edge against your palm. What you're holding is gold – pure gold!

Today, this precious treasure would be worth around £2,000 (which is enough to buy about 40 pairs of trainers or 1,500 massive bags of sweets!). It's called a *bulla*. That's a Latin word (Latin was the main language spoken by the Romans) and it's pronounced the same as bull, only with an 'a' at the end. The names of many round things started with the letters 'bu' or 'beu' back then – and still do today: bump, bush, bubble or bunion (a bunion is a bumpy lump some people get on their feet). This *bulla* looks a bit like a giant gold bubble, doesn't it? Well, that's exactly what it is – *bulla* was the Roman word for 'bubble'.

And this is a bubble with an amazing story.

WHOSE *BULLA* WAS THIS?

In ancient Rome, particular people wore *bullae* (that's the plural of *bulla* in Latin) round their necks. *Bullae* acted as signals, showing everyone that the person wearing them had power. Only Roman boys who had been born free – not enslaved or born as slaves – were allowed to wear something like this.

This *bulla* would have been popped round a boy's neck when they were just nine days old, and showed people that these particular babies were considered more important than those whose families had less money than theirs. At first it might seem a bit strange that children would show how wealthy and powerful they were by wearing a neckace so soon after they were born, but if you think about it, some people do the same today when they wear really showy or expensive jewellery! The *bulla* told the world that the wearer and their family had comfortable lives and were among the richest and most influential in society.

But not every family could afford a *bulla* as expensive as the one you're holding. Lots of *bullae* were made of cheaper materials, like leather, lead, linen, wool or bronze, which was then covered in a thin gold layer. No matter what material they were made of, though, *bullae* were all meant to do the same incredible thing...

GOLDEN MAGIC

You see, the Romans thought that *bullae* were magical and could protect the wearer from ghosts, evil spirits and bad luck. This special power came from an amulet – a good-luck charm, often in the form of a coin or a magic spell – contained inside the *bulla*.

> Some people still use amulets today. The 'evil eye' is an amulet found in many cultures and is said to protect you from evil. (So actually, I think they are more like kind eyes!) You might have seen the eye on jewellery, in art or painted on things like ships.

Bullae were sometimes decorated on the outside with images believed to add even more magical powers. Some had pictures of ferocious Gorgons – half-divine mythical female creatures who had the power to 'petrify' (meaning they could turn into stone) anyone who looked at them. (*Petrus* is the Latin word for 'stone', so if you know someone called Peter or Pete, you can tell them their name means 'stony'!)

The *bulla* you're holding would have originally come with a lovely neck chain made from pearls, porcelain beads and a stone known as heliotrope. This stone was sometimes called 'bloodstone' because of the scarlet flecks inside it and the fact that it reflected a blood-red colour in sunlight. Those stones were chosen not just because they looked awesome; they were actually thought to be magic themselves too.

> A Roman author called Pliny the Elder (who lived from 23 or 24 CE to 79 CE) wrote that Roman sorcerers used bloodstones to make themselves invisible! Other people thought that if you put bloodstones on wounds they would magically heal, which is probably why ancient Roman athletes sometimes carried them to deal with sports injuries.

Now take a look at those lovely gold bobble decorations on the *bulla's* edges. They were made by rolling tiny drops of gold in charcoal. Just think how long it would have taken to make a single *bulla*, adding each of these hundreds of fiddly golden balls all around it. Imagine if you dropped one! A lot of effort must have gone into making just this one piece of jewellery...

This particular *bulla* was made in the second century CE, when the Roman Empire was at its biggest and strongest. Because the empire was so massive and spanned so many countries across the world, we can't know exactly where that glittering gold in your hand originally came from. It could have been from gold mines controlled by the Romans in the countries we now call Spain, Britain, Sudan, Bulgaria, Georgia and Turkey.

This gold is just as bright now as it was when it was first hidden in your garden. Gold is a special metal, because even if it's buried in earth or sand, or dropped into water, it doesn't get rusty or tarnished – it always stays sparkly, shiny and bright. It's why the Romans (and many other ancient civilizations) loved gold jewellery so much – they truly believed it was a magic metal. In fact, this belief goes back as far as the ancient Egyptians, who thought that gold was the teardrops of Ra, their great god of the sun.

This is Ra

WHAT TO WEAR WITH YOUR *BULLA*

The child who wore this *bulla* would also have worn an item of clothing called a *toga praetexta*. In Latin, *toga* means 'something that covers you up', and *praetexta* means 'woven with a border at the edge'. A *toga praetexta* is a long bit of whitish, woollen, semicircular cloth, around four to six metres long. It had a purple edge, and it needed to be wrapped around the person wearing it in quite a complicated way. It wasn't super practical . . . and you weren't supposed to cheat and fix your toga together with a brooch or anything, so there was always a danger it might slip off!

About 600 years before this *bulla* was made, only Roman magistrates (men elected to help run the Roman world) would have worn the *toga praetexta*. The Romans believed the founder of Rome himself, Romulus, originally wore one. By the height of the Roman Empire (from around 1 to 250 CE), the *toga praetexta* had become a special garment worn by most wealthy boys (and some girls too) under the age of 16.

When they reached the age of 16 or 17, boys who wore a *bulla* were allowed to swap outfits to wear a different kind of toga: a *toga virilis*. This roughly translates to 'manly toga', and it told everyone that the wearer was an adult who could now hold public office – meaning they could do things like decide how towns were run, as well as organize festivals, musicals and even gladiator fights.

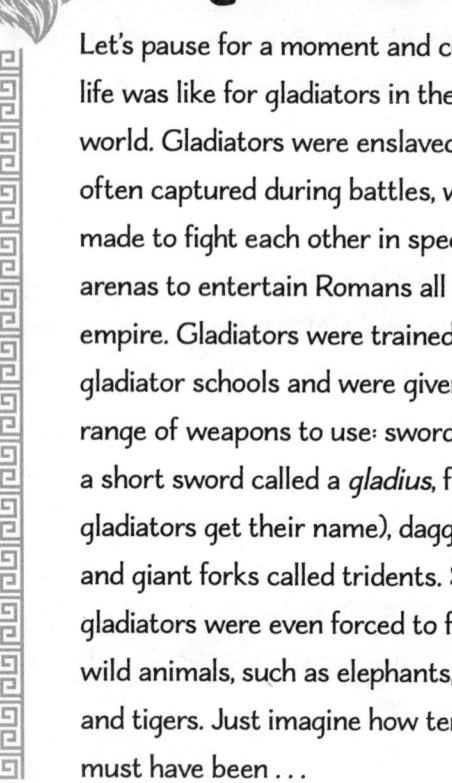

Let's pause for a moment and consider what life was like for gladiators in the Roman world. Gladiators were enslaved people, often captured during battles, who were made to fight each other in specially built arenas to entertain Romans all across the empire. Gladiators were trained to fight in gladiator schools and were given a whole range of weapons to use: swords (including a short sword called a *gladius*, from which gladiators get their name), daggers, nets and giant forks called tridents. Sometimes gladiators were even forced to fight against wild animals, such as elephants, bears, lions and tigers. Just imagine how terrifying that must have been . . .

Once boys reached this grand old age of 16 or 17, when they were judged by society to be men, they donated their *bullae* to their household god. These household gods were called the Lares, and Romans often kept little sculptures of their Lares on the dinner table. They were believed to protect the family home from robbers, and natural disasters like floods, earthquakes and hurricanes.

The idea of having a miniature god on your kitchen table to bring you good luck is interesting, isn't it? It's possible that the child who filled this treasure chest had a Lares at home. It might have been seen as disrespectful to pack the *bulla* away inside a box . . . so I wonder if they said some special prayers or something to their Lares as the special necklace was stored in here for safekeeping?

If you're like me, you might also be wondering why girls didn't get given *bullae* too. It seems unfair, right? Well, just in the corner of the chest over there is another beautiful ancient object, which Roman girls *would* have worn . . .

Go on,
take a look!

This precious twinkling treasure is a bit harder to pick up than the *bulla*, isn't it? It's a lot smaller and more delicate. What you're holding is a *lunula* – a charm in the shape of a crescent moon.

Lunula means 'little moon' and holding this one feels to me as if something precious has fallen from the sky and into my hand. Do you agree? *Lunulae* (the plural of *lunula* in Latin) like this one are particularly rare. We don't tend to find many examples of moon-shaped jewellery in ancient graves or tombs, waiting to be uncovered by historians and archaeologists like me. This is probably because they were not buried with their owners but were instead passed down from one girl to another as a treasured heirloom.

WHOSE LUNULA WAS THIS?

We don't know the name of the girl who originally owned this (although if you'd like to imagine what her name might have been, then Julia, Claudia and Diana were all very popular Roman names that are still used today!) but we do know she would have been from a wealthy family. Similarly to the *bulla*, the *lunula* is a decoration that girls would have worn round their necks or pinned to their dresses, from when they were eight days old until they got married, which was usually by around the age of 20.

In Roman times, there were lots of rules, customs and traditions like this that told women and men, and girls and boys, what they could and couldn't do. In the ancient Roman world you had to act as society expected you to. For example, only the emperor was allowed to be dressed head-to-toe in purple, priestesses were encouraged to wear orange, and this *lunula* could only be worn by girls who weren't foreign or enslaved.

Religion also played a big role in how Romans behaved. (Some language experts say that the word 'religion' comes from the Latin word *religio*, which has links to the word for 'binding', meaning that you are bound to your devotion and obligations.) The Romans' strong religious beliefs and their strict rules meant many Romans in the past all tended to have a similar understanding of the world as one another, and how they were meant to behave. Asking a child if they believed in the Roman gods and goddesses would have been like asking them if they believed in the sea!

So, the little girl who wore this lovely *lunula* was probably very well behaved and did as she was told by society almost all of the time. In fact, children your age would have been expected to follow 'mores' – an ancient Roman word we still use today meaning custom, habit or acceptable behaviour.

DIVINE PROTECTION

Just like the *bulla*, the *lunula* was believed to protect the wearer from harm. This protective magic was thought to be placed into the *lunula* by the Roman goddesses Selene and Diana. Selene and Diana were goddesses of the moon, so it is almost certain the Roman girl who owned this *lunula* would have imagined these divine women watching over her as she went about her day.

Diana was a goddess of hunting, too. That meant she looked after both hunters and the hunted, victors and victims, the strong and the weak; she gave protection to any animal or human that needed and deserved her help.

Imagine being a young girl in ancient Rome, feeling the protection of two powerful goddesses as you wore your little moon! This must have been a wonderfully comforting experience back in the day, don't you think?

The Romans weren't the only people who wore necklaces like this *lunula*. Ancient Greek girls did too, as did the Celts (who lived all over Europe, including the places we now call Ireland, Wales and France), people from Germania, and the Vikings. So, as you hold this piece of ancient Roman jewellery, which is 20 centuries old, it's exciting to think that lots of people throughout the world and history owned and liked very similar beautiful things.

It connects us.

WHERE TO SPOT A LUNULA

There's a place where you can see another *lunula* in action. In modern Rome there's a huge eleven-metre square ancient altar called the Ara Pacis Augustae. It's about the length of a bus! Its name is Latin, and it's pronounced *a-ra pah-kiss au-gust-hi*. It means 'Augustus's Altar of Peace', and it was built to celebrate the first Roman emperor, Augustus (a soldier, as pretty much all Roman emperors were), returning triumphantly to Rome in 13 BCE after a series of battles.

Did you know that the months July and August are named after two Roman rulers? July comes from Julius Caesar (100–44 BCE) and August from Emperor Augustus (63 BCE–14 CE). There are so many clues leading back to the ancient world in our own everyday lives!

The altar is made of beautiful, gleaming carved marble that came from the Greek island of Paros. Originally, before it began to fade, this bright white marble would have been painted with lots of different colours – reds and pinks and blues and greens and gold. It's still covered in intricate decorations and carvings: flower garlands, priests and emperors walking in a procession, female warriors, and Pax, the Roman goddess of peace. On one side there is a carving of a little girl peeping out – and she's wearing a *lunula* EXACTLY like the one you're holding.

The Altar of Peace itself wasn't actually a particularly peaceful place, though. People would sacrifice goats, sheep and cows to the gods and goddesses on it, so it would often have been covered in blood!

PASSING DOWN THE LUNULA

As we have already learned, boys left their *bullae* to their household gods when they came of age. So you might be wondering why girls passed their *lunulae* on from one generation to another? And the answer is, we don't really know!

That's one of the reasons I think history is so great:

there are always **new questions** to be answered,

new riddles to be unravelled,

new mysteries to be solved!

Keeping their *lunulae* might have been a way for women to hold on to their wealth. At the time, it wasn't as easy for women to earn their own money or to decide what they did with it, because Roman society was a patriarchy. Patriarchies are societies where a lot of the power is in the hands of the men. So it might be that in a world where men held so much of the wealth and influence, holding on to their *lunulae* was a way for women to retain their own precious pieces of treasure.

Mind You!

Roman women could actually work in business, unlike in some other ancient societies. And many were very successful at it, too. One woman, who was called Lydia, came from what is now Turkey – once part of the Roman Empire – and she ran a very successful business making and trading brightly coloured textiles. She did so well, she even gets a mention in the Bible!

Whatever happened to most *lunulae* when women married, this particular lovely 'little moon' would have passed through many female hands before it ended up buried in this treasure chest, deep underground in your back garden . . .

Let's put the *lunula* back now and see what else we can rummage for. But the next time you look up at the moon, why not take a moment to imagine Diana and Selene up there keeping an eye out for you . . .

OK, so this next object isn't *exactly* a pizza (I can't imagine how mouldy a pizza from thousands of years ago would be today!). But what you have in front of you is a piece of wall with a *painting* of a pizza on it. It's got a bread base, like the modern pizzas we know and love, but tomatoes didn't arrive in Europe until 1,500 years after this was painted, so it would probably have been flavoured with a pesto sauce instead.

I'm not surprised this piece of wall art has been tucked in this chest for safekeeping – it's so beautifully drawn. Ancient Romans didn't have cameras, computers, printers or printing presses, so all their art, crafts and decorations were created by hand. And this artefact proves just how skilled they were – can you see how real the pizza looks?

THE TERRIBLE FATE OF POMPEII

This painting comes from the bustling Roman town of Pompeii, where there were lots of fast-food joints and street-food vendors.

But the town of Pompeii suffered a terrible fate. In 79 CE, a nearby volcano called Mount Vesuvius erupted. The eruption

boomed

across the town, making the ground

shake

and covering the buildings and most of the people living there under millions of tons of ash and pumice (volcanic rock). The effects were so vast that the town was pretty much lost until 1748, when scientists and archaeologists rediscovered its ancient ruins. The layers of ash had helped to preserve many of the buildings and objects that had been buried. This included the Roman version of a cash register, where the owner of a street-food cafe would have counted their earnings for the day!

FAVOURITE FOODS

Perhaps the child who added this painting to the chest loved pizza and wanted to preserve a memory of how it tasted?! It looks like the pizza was topped with date and pomegranate. Or it could be a kind of herby, spicy cheese that looks a bit like pineapple! There's also a glass of wine in the background.

> I think the very best pizzas are made in Italy – especially when cooked with ingredients from the countryside around Pompeii. The soil there is really fertile, because of the minerals and ash that settles after Mount Vesuvius erupts ... It has done this lots of times – there have been at least 54 eruptions over the last 10,000 years. The fruit, vegetables and wheat that grow in the region, called Campania, are beautifully rich and tasty as a result. So, whatever was on that ancient pizza, we know it would have been delicious.

Let's dive back into the chest now and learn more about the day-to-day life of the child who buried these unusual treasures.

As well as the wafts of the delicious smell of pizza circling around Roman towns, there would also have been the sound of music everywhere. The Romans just loved music. They had musicians to accompany lots of events in their lives: chariot races, dinners, processions and religious festivals. For people who had musical skills, there were always plenty of opportunities to perform!

The Roman music scene helps us to understand that curious-looking thing over there resting up against the side of the chest. I know, it looks like a giant baby's rattle, doesn't it? Well in some ways, that is exactly what it is! It's called a *sistrum*, which, in ancient Greek, means something that was shaken and jangled.

THE MAGIC OF MUSIC

These *sistra* (the word for lots of *sistrums* in Latin) were special musical percussion instruments often played by women and young girls. They make a really eerie **shooshhing** kind of noise and were believed to help ward off evil spirits. (The Romans seemed very worried about the evil spirits all around them, didn't they?!)

Young, female *sistra* players were sometimes followers of the powerful ancient Egyptian goddess Isis.

This is Isis ▶▶▶▶▶

Isis was thought to protect ordinary people if they said the right spells and prayers in her name. The Romans, who adopted the goddess as part of their own religion, believed Isis helped guide the dead to the afterlife. Roman girls in particular – both rich and poor – seemed to have loved worshipping Isis because she was said to contain all feminine divine powers in the world. You can find ancient paintings of Isis actually carrying a *sistrum* herself.

If you look closely, that decoration on the top is of a

mother cat with her little kitten beside her. The cat's probably there because the Egyptians loved cats (they even worshipped them as gods!).

I love the idea that a girl, maybe about the same age as you, would have got to play one of these, and to sing hymns, and to think about a powerful goddess who might protect her.

Religious rattles like this one have been found in Roman sites in London, France and Germany, and by the third century CE, Isis was worshipped in pretty much every town in the Western Roman Empire. I wonder where the one that's ended up in the bottom of your garden originally came from? If you shake it, it still makes a beautiful sound 2,000 years after it was first made.

By the way, while you're looking inside the chest for the next wonder, I'll just mention another musical instrument that I'm NOT surprised isn't in that chest – because it was just so huge: **the Roman horn.** These things were

enormous!

They were like giant, hollow circles and could be 1.5 metres wide. Men would carry them on their shoulders to use for making announcements in big public spaces, for example calling people to come to listen to a proclamation in a town square or encouraging soldiers to go into battle to fight.

They looked a bit like this.

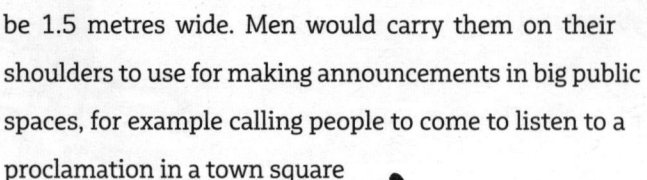

Imagine trying to carry that on your back – I'd rather have the *sistrum*! Or a little whistle instead. Romans would make these from terracotta (baked clay), in the shape of birds. These whistles didn't cost a lot to produce, so it's likely that they were popular with Roman children, who would have filled the streets and gardens of Rome with the piping sound of birdsong.

Let's see what else we can find inside the chest. What about that intriguing thing that looks like a miniature castle, a sandcastle or a model fort?

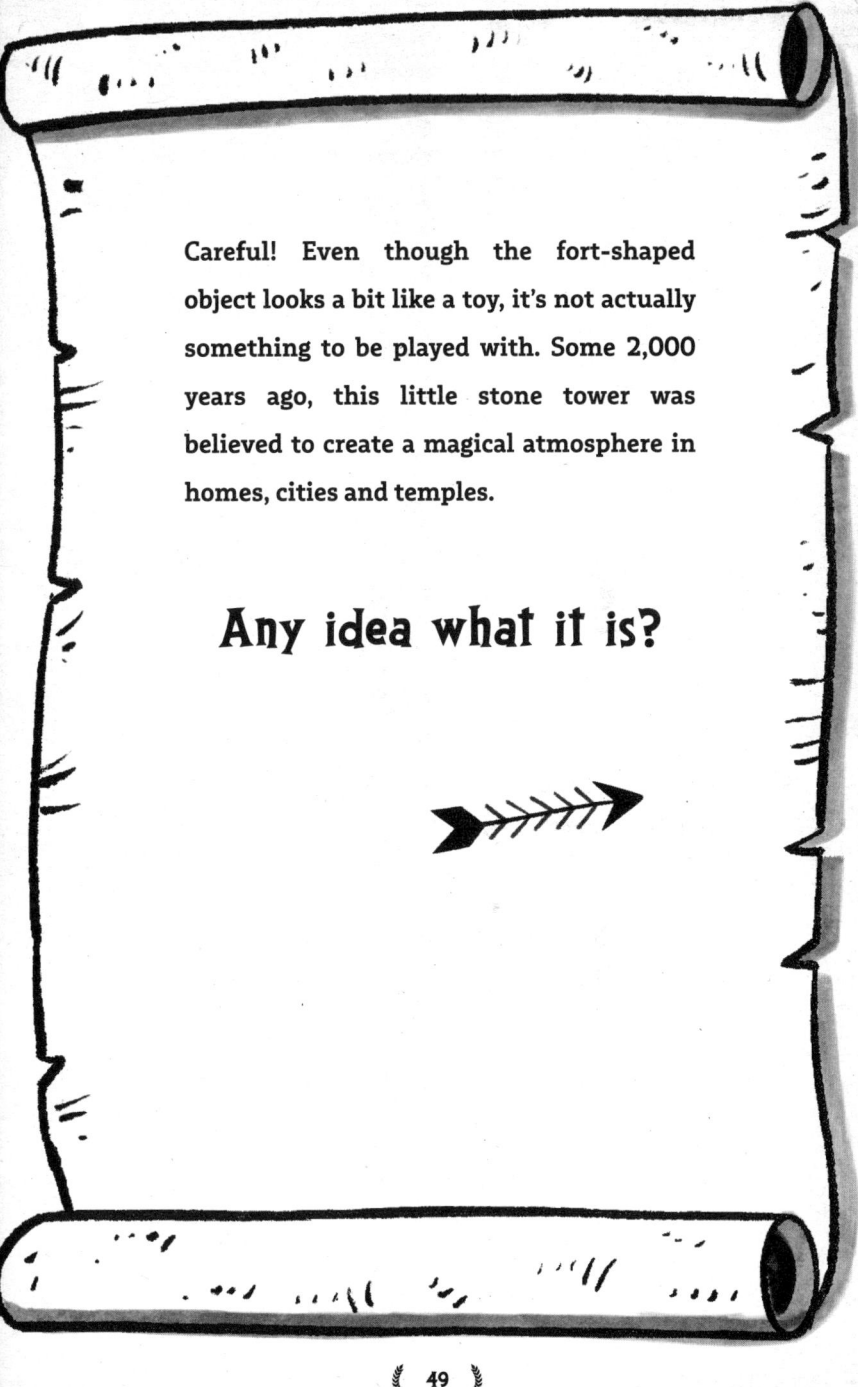

Careful! Even though the fort-shaped object looks a bit like a toy, it's not actually something to be played with. Some 2,000 years ago, this little stone tower was believed to create a magical atmosphere in homes, cities and temples.

Any idea what it is?

SWEET SMELLING SMOKE

It's an incense burner! This one is in the shape of a fort because ancient incense was so precious it was often kept carefully guarded under lock and key. Romans had incense burners in lots of shapes, like shallow bowls – similar to the ones you might eat cereal from now – or decorated birds or priestesses holding up giant saucers on their heads. There was a whole industry dedicated to making these burners – because for the Romans, incense really, really mattered. Burning incense was believed to help take messages up to the gods as its smoke billowed into the sky.

The word incense actually comes from the Latin *incendere* ('to burn'). Incense is harvested very carefully from under the bark of a rare tree called the *Boswellia sacra*, which only grows in a few countries, such as Oman, Yemen and Somalia. When you gently chip and scrape the bark to get incense sap out, it looks as though sticky drops of milk are oozing from the tree trunk. The tree sap feels a bit like white glue, and when it is dried it turns a golden colour. The magic happens when a blob of this frankincense (frankincense is basically the poshest and most expensive kind of incense you can get) is placed on hot charcoal: it slowly burns and releases billows of gorgeous, bittersweet-smelling smoke. In fact, the word 'perfume' comes from this burning process – *per fumum* in Latin means 'through smoke'.

THE MANY USES OF INCENSE

The Romans believed these wafts of richly scented smoke would make the gods more likely to listen to their pleas. Romans asked for many things; for instance, to be blessed with a good harvest, to be lucky in love or to be kept safe from their enemies. So, if you were a child living in ancient Rome, you'd have walked around the streets with the smell of incense hanging thick in the air – thick with hope.

Incense also had (and still has) many

practical uses. It's an insect-repellent – mosquitoes, flies and spiders hate the smell. It was added to eyeliner, a make-up product people have been using for thousands of years to draw dark lines around their eyes. Ancient Romans – especially those who lived in Egypt – added incense gum to their black eyeliner to make it thicker and stickier. It was also incredibly useful as a medicine, a skin cleanser, and, because it was so sticky, incense was sometimes even used to plug wounds.

People also loved incense because it improved living conditions. Packed tight with people and animals, Roman cities would have smelled **TERRIBLE.** There were all sorts of things left on the streets, from

rotting vegetables and fruit to poo and pee – Yuck!

and sometimes even

DEAD bodies!

Incense would have at least slightly masked all that nasty pong! It was sometimes spread on corpses to make them smell better before they were buried.

Hmmm, interesting!

Incense was used everywhere – from ordinary Roman homes right up to temples. In fact, one of the many objects found preserved among the ruins of Pompeii (which we learned about on page 38) was an incense-burner just like this one. It was found on an altar in the home of a man called Obellius Fermus. We don't know a great deal about him, as not much

else was rescued from Obellius's house, but the home itself was very grand, with lovely columns and marble decorations. We know he was wealthy because in the corner of one of his rooms there was a bronze safe, which would have been used to keep all his cash and treasures in. The bronze was actually melted to the floor by the ferocious force and heat of Mount Vesuvius's eruption.

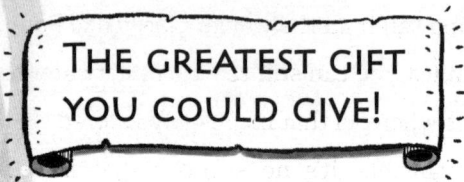

THE GREATEST GIFT YOU COULD GIVE!

As you can see, incense has many uses. What's more, if incense supplies ran out, Roman people genuinely believed they would not be able to communicate with their gods, which would have been a disaster! All of this made incense incredibly valuable – it was worth

more than gold!

The Middle Eastern people who traded it (the Nabateans, some of whom are the ancestors of the modern-day Bedouin, nomadic desert populations who still harvest incense today) became mega-wealthy. The Nabateans would ride over 2,000 miles on camels to bring incense

to Roman traders. The traders would then pack the incense on to boats and sail it all the way to places like Pompeii. In the Bay of Naples, you can still see the underwater remains of warehouses where all that incense was stored.

Being so valuable, it's no surprise that incense was considered a very generous gift. It even features in the Bible, in which we're told the story of the three wise men, who gave the gifts of gold, frankincense and myrrh to the baby Jesus.

What you're looking at is like so many clues from the past:

it can be the simplest objects that have the most interesting stories to tell!

We still use incense today, in churches, temples and homes, to make rooms smell sweeter. Next time you see a incense burner, don't get too close, but take a nice, deep sniff and imagine the Romans inhaling the smell of precious incense. You'll be experiencing the same aromas that girls and boys who lived 2,000 years ago enjoyed. You'll literally be breathing in history!

Now, if you return to the chest, you can see an object whose purpose you can instantly identify, and that has changed very little over thousands of years . . . and I think you're going to love it! It might not be what you would normally think of as treasure, but I think it is SO cool . . .

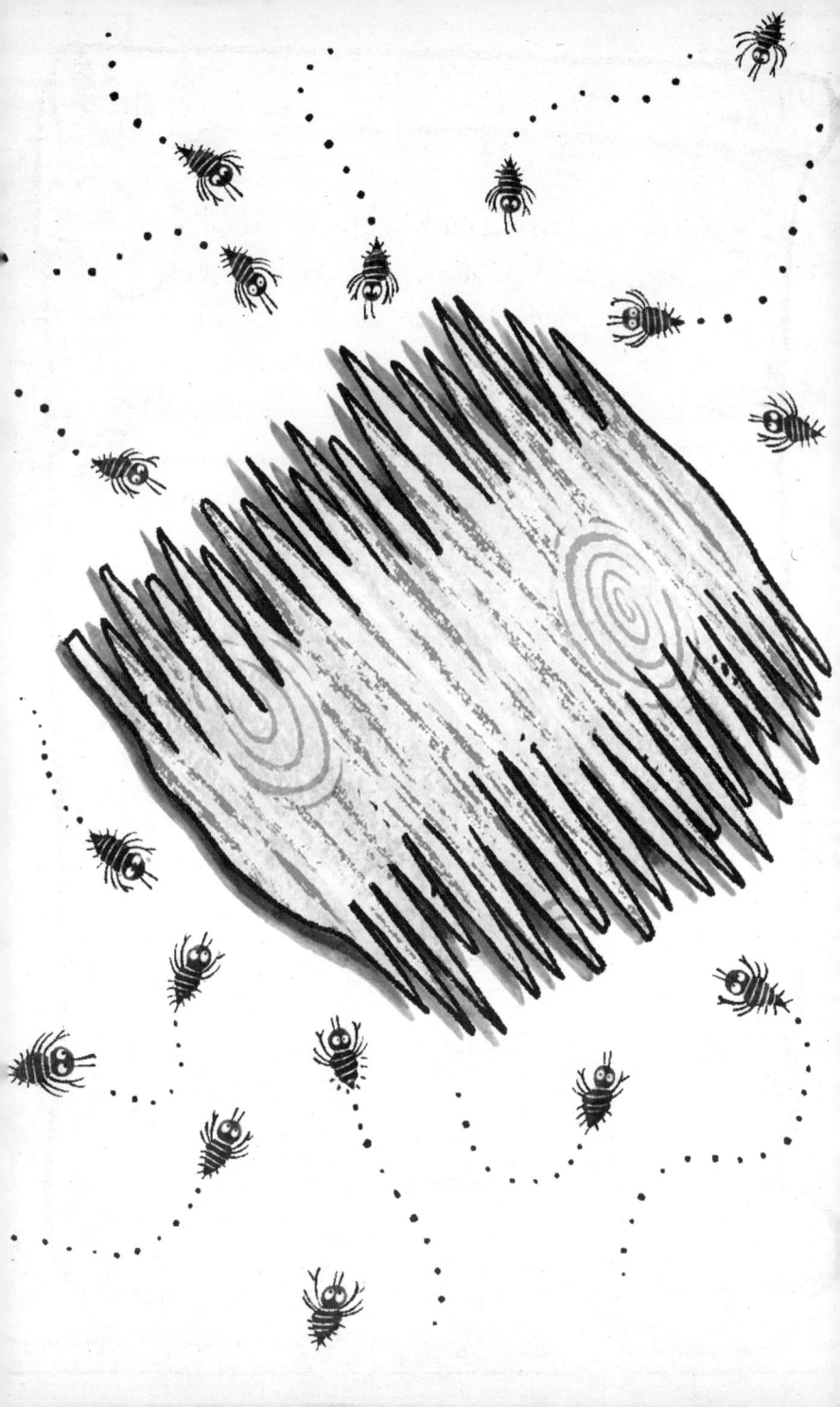

Have you ever had nits? Well, if you have, don't worry – you're not alone. People across the globe and all throughout history have also had to deal with nits! Nits are little eggs, and the insects that lay them are called head lice. Head lice live in human hair (in fact, it's the only place they live!). They don't like to budge, no matter how itchy we feel. In fact, they're one of the most resilient insects in the world – they hang on for dear life using six special claws on the end of each of their six legs.

But fear not!

Humans have worked out clever ways to deal with nits and head lice, and what your hand is hovering over in the chest there is an ancient bit of nit-wrangling technology. Careful when you pick it up – it has teeth, and their edges might still be sharp.

ANCIENT NITS!

This is a nit comb, definitely thousands of years old, and yet it looks **EXACTLY** like the ones we use today. It's even got a bit of ancient hair trapped in its teeth! Isn't that incredible? If you took that hair out and gave it to a scientist, they'd be able to do tests and tell you a whole lot about the person it belonged to, including where they came from and what they liked to eat.

Ancient Roman nit combs were made of wood and sometimes metal. This one is made from boxwood, which is hard, smooth and strong. Look carefully at the middle part and you'll see the original tree rings. (Tree rings are rings inside a tree trunk – each one represents one year of the tree's life.) This particular piece of wood is both bendy and strong – perfect for yanking nits out of hair!

The Romans used boxwood to make many things, including flutes, jewellery chests and even tools for surgeries.

They also believed that boxwood and boxwood leaves could cure illnesses like fevers, malaria (a disease passed on from mosquitoes) and skin ulcers. So, nit combs made from boxwood might also have helped to heal spots and scratches on people's heads (perhaps caused by scratching away those pesky head lice!). Roman cities were *very* crowded, and children often slept in the same rooms as other people: the servants or slaves looking after them, other members of the family, or sometimes guests. And because lice spread by jumping around, they would happily jump from one head to another all night long. Poor children (and grown-ups!) – what with lice bites and flea bites and mosquito bites, they must have been pretty itchy a lot of the time!

Do you remember me talking about the ancient town of Pompeii that was destroyed when Mount Vesuvius erupted? Well, just along the coast from there is another town called Herculaneum that was also destroyed. And because it was even closer to the eruption it was ferociously hot when the volcano exploded. The wave of fierce heat that hit the town was around 550 degrees – hotter than the hottest oven. The preserved remains of one poor woman who sadly died there was found with a metal comb in her hair with nits and lice trapped underneath!

Careful!

Don't drop this next artefact! It's a bottle made of precious glass – 2,000-year-old glass that's still perfectly intact.

If you turn the bottle over, you'll see some sticky stuff in the bottom. That is actual, **real perfume** that has survived from Roman times!

Isn't that incredible?

I'm not surprised this bottle has been stored so carefully in a treasure chest. If we were to remove that bottle plug, we might even be able to smell the scent. Better not though, as it's incredibly delicate and we don't want to ruin it after it has survived so long.

> I was once digging up some ancient remains in Greece, and my friends opened a bottle containing something called 'terebinth' – basically, the ancient equivalent of disinfectant (a strong chemical used for cleaning). We could smell it wafting around the room even though it was 3,500 years old!
>
> Amazing!!

SWEET SMELLS

Romans often used lavender and olive oil in their perfumes. They also used roses and other flowers that they would have grown in their gardens. So even though what you're holding now is a brown, sticky sludge, back then it would have been a liquid that smelled delicious and looked lovely and golden. (In case you're wondering, the difference between perfume and incense is that perfume is a fragrant liquid, and incense is a solid substance that needs to be burned to give off aromatic smoke.)

People would clean themselves with these scented oils, and they would also add them to oil lamps, so they'd give off a sweet odour. Sometimes they were even turned into edible tablets to help people with **bad breath!**

Perfume was often used when someone died. It would make them smell sweet when they were buried, and sometimes it was left with that person in their grave as a parting gift. This small act of kindness was a way of family and friends saying a bittersweet goodbye to their loved ones.

A PRICEY PERFUME

That amazing bottle you're holding would have been really expensive. In today's money it might have cost anything between £500 and £1,000. This is because it would have taken around **20,000 rose petals** to make a single bottle of perfume like this one. Enslaved people working in perfume factories would have boiled up bag upon bag of freshly collected rose petals in water and then squeezed the oil out of the rose water that was left. There were lots of perfume factories all across the

Roman world, because populations in ancient Rome loved perfumes – from very wealthy people to the poor people who could hardly afford it. One Roman emperor called Tiberius (42 BCE–37 CE) was said to have spent around

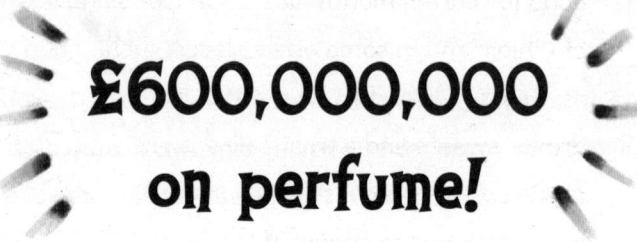

£600,000,000 on perfume!

Even the plug used to close this bottle in your chest would have been pricey. It's made of a substance called mastica, which is the resin that oozes out of mastic trees, many of which were found on the Greek island of Chios. Mastica hardens as it dries to form 'tears' that are a sort of yellow, milky colour. But when the resin oozes out of the bark of the mastic tree it looks like hundreds of tiny, crystal-clear diamonds are dripping out.

The Romans also used mastica as a kind of chewing gum – it tastes (and smells) delicious, it whitens teeth and it is even good for curing mouth ulcers. On the island of Chios (and in some other places, such as Turkey), they still use mastica to flavour drinks, sweets and a treat called 'sweets of the spoon', which is like a syrupy jam best eaten by the spoonful! If you ever visit Chios, give it a try and you can experience something a Roman child would have enjoyed 20 centuries ago.

Delicious!

The glass of the perfume bottle looks a bit like a rainbow, don't you think? Romans loved brightly coloured things. They invented a technique called 'iridescence', named after Iris, the Greek goddess of rainbows, to make glass glisten and gleam with lilac, pink, purple and green colours. If you hold up iridescent glass it has a wonderful, pearly kind of gleam to it. We still produce iridescent glass today – thank you, Romans, for your clever idea!

It's incredible, isn't it, that this bottle has been lost for hundreds of years, and yet it hasn't got a single chip in it – not a single crack. The original owner must have looked after it really well ...

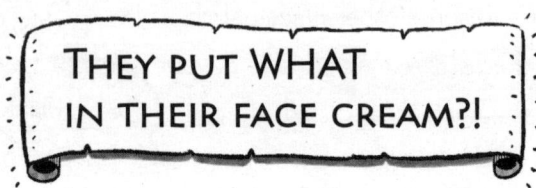

THEY PUT WHAT IN THEIR FACE CREAM?!

In Roman homes, this perfume would have been stored along with other popular beauty treatments, like goose-fat face cream that was supposed to be lovely and moisturizing, tweezers for plucking hairs out of ears or noses or chins, little scoops to get wax out of ears, and even face-whiteners made of **human pee** (because urine contains a natural bleach!).

Gross!

Having placed the perfume bottle very carefully back in its spot, it's time to move on. This next item is easy to find! It's just as well the treasure chest is so big, or the Roman child who packed it up would never have been able to fit this next ancient wonder in!

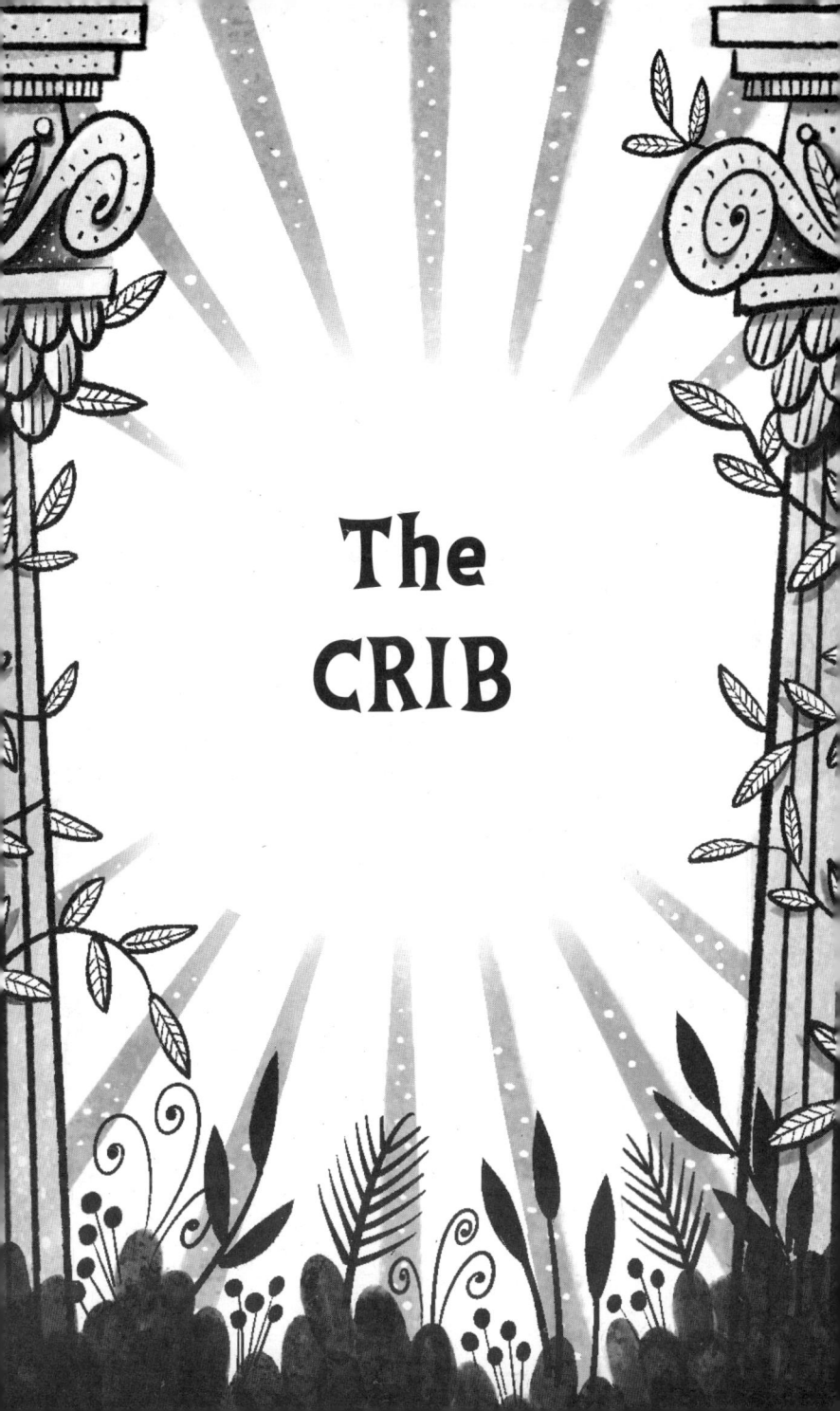

This 2,000-year-old treasure is a crib, just like the cribs people use today to put babies in to sleep. It was made from solid oak and manufactured to a very high standard, so it probably belonged to a wealthy family.

As babies can be a bit **pongy** sometimes, Romans often stuffed crib mattresses with hay, which would soak up any odours of **poo** and **wee.** So, cribs and cradles in Roman homes would have smelled a bit like a horse's stable! To mask this, Romans also placed herbs and sweet-smelling leaves such as myrtle in their mattresses to make them smell nicer.

WHERE DID THE ROMANS LIVE?

Roman houses could be two or three storeys high, and in big cities like Rome there were even multi-storey apartment blocks. Poor people often lived in buildings that were a bit like dormitories, with rows and rows of simple beds lining the floor, the people inside all packed together like sardines. These apartments didn't have kitchens or bathrooms or anything. All the cooking and cleaning and washing would be done outside. There wasn't really an idea of privacy in the ancient world – and particularly in ancient Rome! It must have been awful if you were a naturally shy person, mustn't it?

TIME FOR BED!

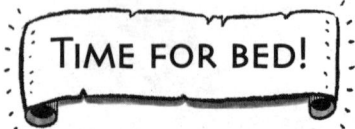

This crib was portable, so it could be moved anywhere. This would have been very handy, because in wealthy families, Roman babies slept in the same room as the servants or enslaved people who worked in the house, rather than in with their parents. Sometimes cribs in posh homes were left in the kitchen beside the warmth created by the cooking fires . . .

That doesn't sound very safe at all, does it?

Rocking babies can help them get to sleep, and this cradle was designed to rock on those curved bits of wood at the bottom. Often strings of charms or amulets (remember them from inside the *bulla*?) were draped across the crib, or even across the baby's chest, to make a jingling sound to soothe them to sleep.

Bigger beds, for young people about your age, have been found in Herculaneum (remember – the whole town that was one of the victims of Vesuvius). They look like they would have been moved around between different rooms too. Would you like to be able to move your bed and sleep in different places each night?

Don't these treasures get you thinking all about the daily experiences of people who lived so long before us . . .?

Baby toys

Nestled in the corner of cribs like this might be some special toys that Roman babies played with. One Roman favourite was a rattle. These came in all shapes and sizes – some looked like mothers and babies having a cuddle together, some were shaped like animals – chickens and pigs, for example – and some even looked like monsters, including one very strange creature – a bird with the antlers of a stag! To make the rattling sound, little clay balls, seeds or sometimes even wolf's teeth were placed inside! The ancients found all kinds of clever ways to use the products of the natural world.

Now . . . what are those in the corner of the chest? They look strange, don't they? Let's see what **mysteries** of the past they'll reveal to us, shall we?

Are you ever bored? I can't say for certain, but I don't think Roman children like the one who packed up this treasure chest were ever bored. In fact, there isn't even a Latin word for boredom!

Life was busy (and pretty hard) for children – and for most grown-ups, too. Just think about it: with no phones and no computers, most young people would have been doing chores and running errands for a lot of the day, taking messages from one shop owner to another, from their parent to a friend, looking after young siblings or farm animals, or harvesting crops or whizzing messages out to another family member working in the fields.

What?!

But one of the more unusual treasures in this chest of yours gives us a clue about something we know Roman children loved to do if they had a second to spare...

LET'S PLAY!

During any time off, they would probably have played games with friends or by themselves. We know this because lots of children's games have been discovered when historians have been digging for history. And there are many carvings and paintings of Romans (both adults and children) playing games too. These include pushing hoops along with a stick, using homemade swings dangling from the branches of a tree, or playing board games where the boards were carved into paving stones in streets. If you walk down one street called Port Street, which originally led to the harbour of an ancient city called Ephesus (in what is now modern-day Turkey), you can see tons and tons of circular board games carved into the stones of the road. You can imagine ancient Romans sitting outside the shops that lined this road playing games while they waited for new customers to come along from the boats that had just docked (800 ships could fit into the harbour of Ephesus at any one time!).

Swimming races were popular with ancient Romans too. Given how much travel in the ancient world was by boat, along rivers and seas, it was a pretty good idea to be a strong swimmer – it would help you avoid drowning if you fell in!

THE RULES OF KNUCKLEBONES

These four strangely shaped objects in the chest were part of a game that children would have played right across the Roman Empire. They all look fairly similar, don't they? But there are small differences between their surfaces. These curious things are called 'knucklebones'. They are actual animal bones (though confusingly, not their knuckles) – taken from the ankles of either pigs, goats or sheep, and Romans used them to play a game.

Do you want to have a go at playing the ancient game of knucklebones?

Go ahead and pick them up.

Knucklebone rules

1. **Throw all** the knucklebones into the air (but not too high or you might lose them!).

2. **Look carefully** at how they've landed on the ground.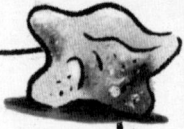

3. If most of the knucklebones have fallen with a **different side turned up** to the others, then you've done really well – it means you've got a high score.

The best throw was when each upturned side of the knucklebones was different. This winning throw was called a **'Venus'**. It was called that because Venus was a goddess who was thought to be lucky (we'll hear more about her later). Throwing a Venus was like throwing two dice and getting the number six on both!

THE MANY USES OF KNUCKLEBONES

Knucklebones were not just used for games; Roman women also used them to communicate with the goddess Venus and pray to her. To do this, a woman would throw them into the air and pray that they landed in a certain way. If they did, she'd believe Venus was replying to say that she'd help her answer her prayers.

This is Venus

Roman men gambled with knucklebones too. There are 35 different possible ways that the knucklebones could land, and groups of gamblers would bet their money on what the results of the throws might be. Romans loved gambling, and they sometimes did so with silver coins called *denarii*.

In places like Jordan and the United Arab Emirates, coins are still called *dinars* after these ancient Roman coins.

We still have games like this today. One example is 'skipjacks'. To play, you throw a little ball in the air, and the aim of the game is to pick up as many metal 'jacks' (which have knobbles on the end a bit like knucklebones) as you can before catching the ball. I wonder if ancient children would have played a similar game using a small ball, and knucklebones in place of jacks? I'll have to keep looking for ancient evidence to find out.

Fortunately for the children in ancient Rome, they didn't ONLY have old bones as toys to play with. If you peer deeper inside the chest, you'll see lots more toys, some more friendly looking than others!

Can you see that tiny arm sticking out of the chest? Let's look at that next. The arm is made of oven-baked clay, so it's pretty sturdy. It belongs to a doll whose arms and legs can be moved – just like many of the dolls we have today. Roman children dressed their dolls up in clothes, brushed their hair and even, if they came from a really rich family, gave them special doll-sized pieces of jewellery made from real gold!

Less wealthy families had cheaper toys made of material that hasn't survived the centuries very well. However, one rag doll was found in Egypt from the time when the Romans were in charge there. It survived because the dry desert sands of Egypt are amazing at preserving things. The doll was made of wool, linen and papyrus (papyrus is a kind of reed that grows along the River Nile, which Ancient Egyptians used to write on).

There are some more toys in here, too. Dig in a bit deeper, why don't you – and see what else you can find!

MOVING TOYS

Many wealthy families and their children lived in the capital of the empire: Rome itself. They may have walked past the Colosseum, an enormous amphitheatre in the centre of Rome where gladiator fights happened, or the Pantheon, a great round temple dedicated to all the Roman gods and goddesses. You can still go inside the Colosseum and the Pantheon today. Or maybe they walked past the Circus Maximus, where exciting, fast-paced and dangerous chariot races took place. That's where we get the word **'circus'** from: in Latin, *circus* means 'a round place'.

This is what the Colosseum looks like today!

Inspired by the fights, races and other exciting events that took place in these venues, some toymakers created really fancy toys that actually moved as if they were machines. These were usually bought by wealthy families for their children to play with.

TRAVELLING TOYS

The wealthiest families had lots of different ways of getting around. Some might have been driven around in chariots led by horses. And some were carried in vehicles called 'litters', which were portable beds that were moved along by animals or people! Some mini chariots for children and toddlers would have been pulled along by goats or geese. Yes, geese!

How on earth do you train a goose or goat to pull a chariot?

Well, Romans did it! Though it was only very wealthy families who could afford something like that.

This chariot and horse toy looks just like the kind that rich families would've been transported around in. The horse has wheels and would have been pulled along the ground by the child playing with it.

Roman children also had larger chariot toys, with rotating wheels, just like the real ones that raced round the Circus

Maximus. These were often bright red – and many that still survive today are just as bright and vivid as they once were! Red was a favourite colour of Mars, the Roman god of war. Perhaps their toy chariots were supposed to look like the red chariots used by the Roman army? That's likely, because the Romans were pretty belligerent (that's a punchy word for 'aggressive', by the way. It comes from the Latin *bellum*, which means 'war').

ROWDY ROMANS

The Romans had huge armies and enjoyed fighting in all forms. So, it's no surprise that they had some less friendly looking toys too. That next object in the chest is a wooden dagger. It might have been used by boys to practise with, as if they were real soldiers (in fact, many Roman poets wrote about boys fighting with wooden daggers just like this one). This is because lots of Roman boys grew up to become soldiers. When the Roman Empire was first expanding under the Emperor Augustus, every male Roman citizen over a certain height (see page 137) was expected to fight in the army between the ages of 16 and 46.

Girls weren't allowed to be soldiers or to fight in battles – the Romans thought that was a job for men. (Although I have seen some ancient graves from Roman times in a region called the South Caucasus – where the countries Azerbaijan, Armenia and Georgia are – where women have been buried with weapons and it looks as though they have battle wounds on their bones, so maybe some women did train to fight at this time . . . but probably against the Romans rather than with them!)

> Although Roman women and girls didn't normally fight, there is a fascinating marble carving that shows two female gladiators battling against each other. The carving originally came from the ancient city of Halicarnassus in what is now Turkey and is now on display in the British Museum. One of the gladiators was called Amazonia, like the mythical warrior women known as the Amazons. The other was called Achilleia after a famous Greek hero called Achilles, who was extremely good at fighting.

And if you didn't want to play with knucklebones, dolls, daggers or hoops, and you couldn't afford mini chariots, or horses on wheels, there were always spinning tops, which are just the same as the ones used today. In fact, children were playing with toys like this as far back as the eighth century BCE – 300 years or so before the Romans.

All of this is a reminder that so many of the games we play and the things we do today were actually created by Romans and other ancient societies many centuries ago!

It's time to put the toys away now. Let's move on to more cool, school-ey things.

We've talked a lot about how the Romans could be pretty aggressive, and how they violently took over lots of other peoples' land. Well, all that is true and it's important that we don't forget it. However, it is also worth bearing in mind that the Romans conquered with both the pen AND the sword. (Well, usually with the sword first, then the pen.)

DEAR DIARY...

Romans loved to write. They kept diaries and made notes and logs about what they were doing, including:

- **Who they were trading with**
- **Who they were fighting**
- **Who they'd arranged to meet for a meal**
- **Who they were visiting on holiday**
- **And what shopping they were planning to buy that day . . .**

They wrote down pretty much everything!

They also loved writing song lyrics and plays and long histories about how brave and clever Romans could be.

So brave!

So brainy!

So strong!

Although about 15 per cent of people living in the Roman Empire were literate (which means they could read and write), lots of writing in Roman times was done by Greek slaves. And not every child was able or even allowed to read and write. Enslaved children were almost never taught to read. But if you came from a well-to-do family, it was a badge of honour if you could read and write from an early age. As a child, you would often be taught at home by one of those Greek slaves, or in a small kind of primary school from the age of about six or seven. There were no free schools – so you only got an education if your family were rich enough to afford it. It's terrible to think of all the talent and opportunity that was wasted through history, isn't it – just because your household couldn't afford to send you to school.

WONDERFUL WORDS

Literate children wrote on special tablets. Is that one in the chest? I think it is! What's more, it's still bound up with leather strings, so it might just have its original message inside.

A message that hasn't been read for almost 2,000 years!

Why don't you carefully untie the strings and open it up? What can you see? Some words? What do they say? Read them out:

>>>>>> **FOCUS**

>>>>>> **VIDEO**

>>>>>> **DATA**

>>>>>> **ACTOR**

They may look like modern English words, but they're actually Latin. In that ancient language, *focus* means 'fireplace' or 'hearth' – where light comes from. That's where the meaning for 'focus' comes from, because when we walk into a room, our focus naturally goes to the fireplace. *Data* means 'something to start calculating with' and *video* means 'I see' – which is what you do when you watch a video.

Actor is the one word here that is almost exactly the same in Latin and English. In Latin it means 'a doer' (someone who does something), but it was also used in the same way we use it today (to describe a person who acts).

About half of the words you speak every day have their roots in ancient Greek and Latin. It means the past is always with us.

Maybe the child who wrote this list was practising their spelling? We know they had spelling tests in Roman times. Archaeologists have discovered pieces of pottery with spelling tests on, and scraps of papyrus preserved in the sands of Egypt with lists of words written in ink made of soot and burnt oak! Nobody escaped spelling tests and maths lessons, even in Roman times!

Grab a pen and a piece of paper and imagine you're writing on the other side of the tablet on the fresh wax. I'll tell you what to write:

>>>>>> **INDEX**

>>>>>> **ITEM**

>>>>>> **AREA**

These are more pure Latin words that we use every day in English. In Latin, *index* means 'a discoverer' or 'someone who indicates something' – perhaps by pointing with their index finger! *Item* means 'in addition', and *area* means 'an empty piece of level ground'. So, if you say to someone, 'Don't go into that area,' you're using a Latin word!

Tools for writing

Let's look a little closer at the writing tablets. They were made by covering a shallow frame of wood (sometimes boxwood, the same as the nit comb) with a layer of beeswax.

Using a pointed stick called a *stilus* (in France they call pens *stilos* after *stilus*) you could carve words into the wax.

The great thing about this design was that you could easily remove any mistakes from the wax or clear all your work and start afresh. You just had to make the beeswax melt a bit by swooshing a flame over it or leaving it out in the hot sun. Then you rubbed the melted wax until it was smooth with either your thumb or the blunt end of the *stilus*.

Romans who lived close to the Mediterranean also wrote on papyrus from Egypt (see page 88). And if there wasn't a supply of papyrus, you could write on parchment, which was made from animal skin. You could even use old scraps of pottery to write on.

The ancients were very nifty with their recycling!

Roman pupils sometimes used ink, which was often made of 'lamp-black'. Back then, light was provided by flaming torches or lamps, which used animal fat or olive oil as fuel. This all left behind a LOT of soot, or lamp-black, which was then used to make ink.

Towards the end of the Roman Empire, people might have used a thing called oak gall, made from the little knobbly bits on oak trees known as oak apples. Oak apples are full of tannin – that's the brown chemical also found in tea that can stain your teeth. Mixed with incense and iron oxide, the tannin made a gooey black liquid – an ink that was used right across the Roman world. Other materials they used for ink included old wine (which must have smelled horrible and sour), or ink from a squid or even sometimes from a kind of cuttlefish called a sepia (the ink of the sepia is in a little sac just close to its gills, so unfortunately the sepia fish has to be killed to get the ink out). The pens the Romans dipped into all these different kinds of inks were usually made of river reeds.

They had coloured inks too, which were used for different things. Red ink was often used for main headlines

– chapter titles in a book, for example. Purple ink was used for important letters and documents. It was made from sea snails and was so expensive to produce that the colour purple became linked with royalty! If an emperor was too young to rule by himself, his official guardian would use green ink to sign documents on his behalf.

Romans also wrote with invisible ink when they wanted to communicate secretly. They wrote secret messages with lemon juice, myrrh (another tree resin, like frankincense) or egg white. These substances stay invisible until they are heated up, usually by carefully passing a candle underneath the papyrus or parchment. The heat causes invisible ink to go brown, allowing the reader to see the message.

There were actually secret police in ancient Rome called the *frumentarii*. These men worked as private detectives or secret agents for the emperor. Their official job was to act like a kind of postal service around the empire, delivering messages, including secret ones, and listening in on conversations.

Pssst!

Pssst!

Pssst!

The ancient Greeks used a far more extreme trick. When they wanted to get a secret message to a king, they tattooed the message on to a poor slave's head and when they shaved off their hair, the message underneath could be read!

> In Britain, near the border with Scotland, there is an ancient place called Vindolanda. It was a Roman military camp where soldiers and their families lived, and it was so boggy that many things that were dropped in it have survived to this day.

You know I said earlier how deserts are great for preserving things because they are so dry? That is certainly true. However, certain kinds of bogland are also special because they contain very little oxygen. This lack of oxygen means that the bacteria that cause decay can't survive, and so more historical treasures survive for us to learn from.

Because of this, lots of ancient treasures have been found in Vindolanda. These include

>»> **leather tents**

>»> **leather boxing gloves**

>»> **a sword still in its case**

>»> **a nail-cleaning kit**

>»> **and even a wooden loo seat!**

(WOW!)

Excitingly, postcards that were written and sent by Romans have been found too. The writing is on thin wooden slips, and these were probably delivered by a child running errands, just like we were talking about earlier.

How amazing – 1,800-year-old postcards!

The postcards tell us about women inviting each other to parties, and children practising writing and grammar on tablets. One poor boy writing on one of these thin strips of wood had been marked harshly by his teacher, who just wrote *SEG* – it's short for *segitur*; Latin for 'sloppy'.)

So much for sitting down, reading and writing, but what about walking around? What did Romans wear on their feet while they did all that marching, fighting, visiting one another, shopping, doing errands and conquering? Let's find out.

Have you ever lost a shoe? Or seen babies lose shoes when their feet are dangling out of a pram and the person pushing hasn't noticed – plop, off the shoe goes! Well, these lost shoes in the treasure chest look quite modern, don't they? A bit like ones that could have been lost on the street outside today. But no: they're Roman and have survived pretty much perfectly across 18 centuries.

CHOOSE YOUR SHOES

Let's take a close peek at one of the shoes. It looks just like a slipper, and because it was made to fit the wearer like a glove it would have been as comfortable as a slipper too! This treasure is made of leather that looks like fishnet.

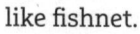

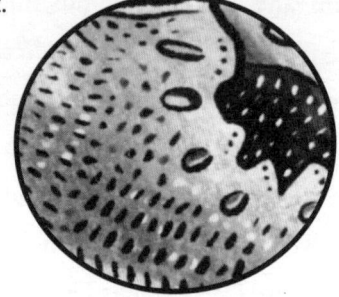

Crocheting those strands of thin leather together required time and skill, so it was a very expensive item of clothing. This little shoe definitely belonged to the toddler of a family who had a lot of money.

Many perfectly preserved shoes have been found in Vindolanda (the place we learned about in the last chapter). So far, around **5,000** have been discovered, and every time archaeologists get to work there, they find more! They have dug up hobnail boots, which have nails fitted in the soles and would have been worn by soldiers. They have also found slip-on shoes with patterned studs

on the bottom, which would have been worn by women. And they have excavated pointy-toed shoes for the fashionable Romans, as well as sturdy boots for walking during a cold British winter.

Roman children would usually wear sensible sandals in the summer, and soft boots that looked a bit like desert boots for when it was rainy or cold out.

Do you have any shoes that look like these?

There's even a perfectly preserved Roman sock still around today. It's bright red and called a toe-sock, which means the toes are all individually separated so they can be worn with flip-flop-style sandals. This sock was preserved by the sands of Egypt, which means 1,800 years ago it was fashionable to wear socks and sandals!

Sadly, not everyone got to wear shoes, and the next item belongs to a person who would most likely have had to go barefoot.

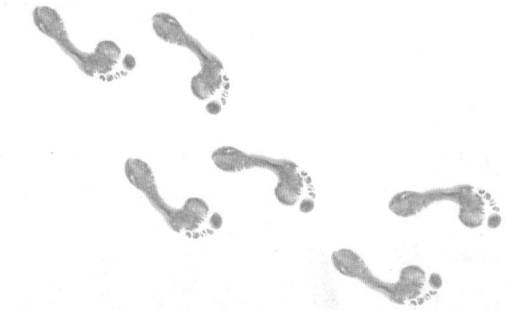

TENEMENE
FVGIAETREVO
CAMEADDOMNVM
EVVIVENTIVMIN
ARACALLISTI

This engraved metal object is gruesome proof that if you'd lived in Rome in 25 CE, many of the men, women and children around you would have been enslaved. The text on this tag reads: *Hold me, lest I flee, and return me to my master Viventius on the estate of Callistus.*

SLAVERY IN ANCIENT ROME

In ancient Rome there was about one enslaved person for every two 'freeborn' (the name given to someone who was born free and not into slavery). Enslaved people were bought and sold as if they were pieces of furniture. They came from countries that are now in Europe, Asia and Africa – anywhere the Romans managed to get to and violently invade.

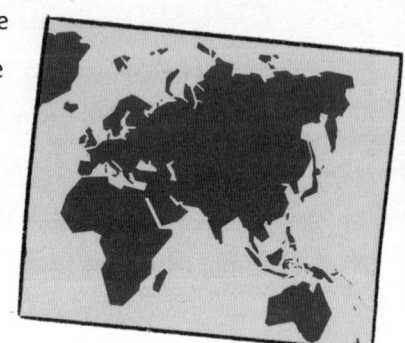

We can't know the exact numbers, but there's a Greek island called Delos that used to be part of the Roman Empire where we're told by authors writing at the time that

10,000 people a day were traded into slavery.

These would have been people who had been stolen from their homes or captured during a war or traded by pirates.

I've seen the round stone pits where some of these poor people were kept. They are like pens for keeping cattle in, only horrifyingly, these were for humans. The pits are under the sea now, but you can still see them through the waves. The slave merchants would have walked around on the ground above these pits, choosing which slaves to buy. Isn't that a terrible thought?

WHAT'S YOUR NAME?

This object is a slave tag, and it would have been one of the very few possessions belonging to the enslaved person.

TENEMENE
FVGIAETREVO
CAMEADDOMNVM
EVVIVENTIVMIN
ARACALLISTI

Enslaved people often had their names taken away and were commonly referred to on their tag only by the job they were forced to do or where they came from. Some tags would read **DOMESTICUS**, which is where our word 'domestic' comes from. A *domesticus* was someone who belonged to the household – so they'd have been given jobs like cleaning, baking, buying household supplies and mending things. They were basically a dogsbody who did whatever they were ordered to do to keep the house running smoothly. Other slave tags have the word

UTILIS on them, meaning 'useful person', or ***AFRICANUS***, meaning a person from Africa.

Imagine having your name taken away and being given a label instead?

Other tags that have been left behind by the Roman Empire say things like, 'If I run away, send me straight back home to my master.' It's just awful what some people chose to do to others. This has happened to enslaved people throughout history and across the continents. Let's take a moment to think about all of them.

Let's see what else is left to discover. It looks like there's a painting in there, or maybe even two, standing up against the chest's back wall . . .

These sturdy painted blocks of wood showing children are called mummy portraits. Interesting name, right? So where did they come from? Well, the pictures come from Egypt and were made when the Romans controlled North Africa. The Romans were in Egypt for around 400 years, and at one point this beautiful country was described as the 'breadbasket of Rome'. This is because the River Nile (which at 6,650 kilometres is the longest river in the world) as it flows through Egypt, floods and creates rich and fertile land on its banks. That fertile soil either side of the River Nile produced huge amounts of wheat – as well as other lovely things like dates (if you sail down the River Nile today its banks are still lined with beautiful date-palm trees). Its wheat was shipped all over the Roman Empire to be made into bread for feeding Rome's citizens.

We need to be careful when handling objects like these. The paint on these artefacts is around 1,700 years old, and it could so easily flake off. It would be terrible to lose or damage a scrap of that. In fact, there are specialist professionals called **art restorers** who spend their lives repairing ancient paintings that have been damaged during wars or natural disasters or have just suffered wear and tear over time. I've always thought that must be such a satisfying job – tending to something beautiful and interesting and making it whole again.

Queen Cleopatra was Egypt's last pharaoh. She was highly intelligent and spoke nine languages, including one used by Troglodyte people who mainly lived in caves – 'troglodytes' in Greek comes from *troglo* ('cave') and *dyein* ('to go into'). After she died, the Romans took over Egypt and it became what's called a province. Provinces were areas outside Italy that were controlled by Rome, usually run by Roman rulers called governors. The Romans LOVED Egypt; in fact, many people from the ancient world adored it. If something was 'made in Egypt' (and some items in the ancient world did have such labels – things like expensive vases, or wall decorations made of inlaid turquoise stone, or lovely little perfume boxes, or plates made of a fine stone called alabaster that lets the light through) it was a mark of high quality, something that was particularly desirable.

Ancient Egyptian artists were particularly good at painting mummy portraits. That picture you're holding was made in a region on the Nile called Fayum, so it's called a Fayum mummy portrait. If you travel up the Nile to Fayum by boat, you'll hear frogs singing like they're in a choir, and the soft hiss of palm trees waving in the breeze. In Roman times you'd have seen blue lotus flowers there too, their petals open and releasing an intoxicating, sweet aroma. Sadly, these are on the verge of extinction in Egypt today. The Nile is such a beautiful place, and the lovely landscape certainly seems to have inspired the many artists who worked there – from ancient times up until now.

So, what exactly is a mummy portrait?

Well, the ancient Egyptians are famous for 'mummification', which is the process of preserving a body after someone has passed away. Mummy portraits are paintings of someone who has died. They were placed on the person's mummified body. They also served as a celebration of the person's life – so they are happy things as well as sad.

WHO'S IN THIS PAINTING?

Right now, you're face-to-face with someone from the past, because that boy in the portrait was a real person, painted from life before he died. Paintings like these are as close as we'll get to a photograph of someone who lived over 1,800 years ago. We know this boy must have had to sit still on a stool or chair for hours while the artist re-created his face on wood.

> Let's try to imagine what it would have been like for him to have that portrait painted.

How long can you sit still on a chair for before you feel like you have to move?

Artists in Roman times used paintbrushes made of things like squirrel hair (and you can still get paintbrushes like this today). Paint was mixed using that gooey-gummy substance called mastica, which made the paint sticky (we talked about mastica on page 68). As we learned, mastica has a lovely smell, so it is likely that as that boy sat for his portrait, he was breathing in and enjoying the smell of the artist's paint. Nice!

> All this talk about paints has reminded me of one of the most amazing things I've ever seen. It was a whole tray of paint pots, full of brightly coloured powder paint, completely undamaged and unchanged since Roman times. It was preserved in an artist's studio at Pompeii.

Let's take a look at the other mummy portrait in your treasure chest. This one's of a teenage girl wearing a gold crown. Only people who worshipped that powerful Egyptian goddess Isis were allowed to wear gold crowns like this –

it was almost like a religious uniform. So, this girl might have been training to be a priestess of Isis before she died.

It's possible that the artist of these portraits was an enslaved person from Greece. After they'd taken over Greek territory in 146 BCE, Romans used Greeks a lot as teachers, artists and letter-writers; the Romans admired the Greeks and were greatly influenced by their culture. There are clues in these mummy portraits that suggest that these children came from wealthy families, so it's likely the enslaved artist came to visit them in their homes, bringing all their paints with them.

DRESSING FOR A PORTRAIT

Can you see that glimpse of a pearl necklace under the girl's top? Hardly anyone in the Roman world could afford to wear jewellery like this! Those pearls might have come from as far away as India, meaning the merchants who traded them had to make long, dangerous journeys by boat across the Indian Ocean, the Red Sea and Mediterranean before selling them in a Roman market. So this girl's family must have had plenty of money to pay the merchants for such rare and sought-after goods.

Children would always dress smartly for their portraits. Sometimes they wore grown-up clothes, more like those that would have been worn by their parents: rich, heavy cloaks and bejewelled clasps, for example. Even if they were wearing children's clothes, such as a simple tunic, they were always the very best one the family owned. That might mean a red woollen cape made with British wool, or linen decorated with gold thread.

The red and black striped dress this girl is wearing is similar to something a man would wear if he belonged to the Roman ruling class called 'senators'. But although she's wearing a dress that must have been chosen to send out a message of power, her expression is very approachable and open, don't you think? Often in these portraits the child is staring straight out at us, so it feels like you're looking directly into their eyes.

FLASHING THE CASH

Commissioning an artist to make paintings like these was a way for wealthy Romans to show off a bit. It allowed them to prove to themselves and their friends how well they were doing in life. Not everyone had art in their homes, and they didn't have things like wallpaper either. Only those with enough spare cash could pay artists to decorate their houses or create moveable portraits like these ones.

One Roman portrait that has been found shows a boy with a very interesting hairdo: his head is completely shaved except for a little curly lock of hair – a bit like a punk rocker! Well, this hairdo is called a 'Horus lock'. (Horus was another powerful Egyptian god and the son of the goddess Isis.) If a child was sick, their head would sometimes be shaved like this. The idea was that if the shaved hair kept growing, they'd recover from their illness. It's interesting the things people in the past believed, isn't it, and how different they are from the things we believe today?

Some mummy portraits have been found in a town with the best name **EVER.**

It's called Crocodilopolis – the City of Crocodiles.

Which leads us very neatly on to our next artefact...

Don't panic.
Don't panic.
DON'T PANIC!

Just move very slowly and carefully and don't look like you're running away. Try to make yourself look **BIG** . . . and remember to breathe. If you breathe, your brain has the oxygen it needs to think. And if you think, you'll have a chance at making the best decision in any crisis.

Quietly now . . .
    actually . . .
        hold on a second . . .
            I think it's OK . . .

On second glance, I don't think that thing in the chest is alive. It's not moving; it's just glinting and gleaming in the light. I don't THINK that's a real crocodile, I think it's just a complete crocodile skin . . .

A SCALY SUIT OF ARMOUR

How strange. It looks like a person's outfit, made from the skin of a crocodile. In fact, what you've found is a suit of crocodile armour.

What a unique bit of treasure!

Whoever created this used the crocodile's front legs to make the armour's arms.

> The words 'arm' and 'armour' come from the same family of words: they're all to do with joining things. Your arm is joined to your body, and armour is usually pieces of metal or leather joined together. Another word we get from 'arm' is 'harmony' - in music, harmony is when different notes are played together to create transporting and beautiful melodies.

Isn't it fascinating to think about a Roman soldier wearing something like this? Crocodile skin is so tough and thick that most lions can't bite through it, so can you imagine how petrifying it would have been to come up against someone wearing this on the battlefield?

They'd have looked like a very well protected monster!

It's quite roomy, too. This was necessary because men could only join the Roman army if they were at least 172 centimetres tall. Why not ask a grown-up to measure you and see if you'd be allowed to join the Roman army once you turn 16 or 17?

That crocodile-skin helmet may have been worn directly on the person's head or perhaps fitted over a metal helmet. Roman (and Greek) soldiers sometimes draped things over their armour to make themselves look as scary as possible. For instance, they might have worn a lion or leopard skin or adorned their helmet with the head of a wild boar. They did this because Hercules, one of their mythical heroes, wore the skin of a lion he had killed so that he looked like a fearsome lion-man to his opponents.

SACRED CROCS

Another crocodile armour suit was found in a place called Manfalut in Egypt. That suit was made right at the end of the Roman Empire, during the third or fourth century CE. It's interesting because we don't know whether that particular crocodile suit was used as armour by a soldier, or by a priest for some kind of religious ritual.

The ancient Egyptians believed crocodiles to be sacred. There's an ancient Egyptian temple, which was later used by the Romans, that was built right on the banks of the Nile in Queen Cleopatra's time. Worshippers, both Roman and Egyptian, would have reached it by boat. It's called Kom Ombo and was built partly in honour of the crocodile. It has lovely carvings of a crocodile-headed God called Sobek all over it, and mummified crocodiles were displayed at the temple's edge. There are even reports that the temple included a pool where crocodiles could swim about.

This is Sobek

There used to be A LOT of crocodiles in the River Nile – around **10,000** – the water must have been thick with them. Almost all the Nile crocodiles have vanished now, because a dam was built between 1960 and 1970 near the Egyptian border with Sudan, which prevents them from swimming into Egypt. I've actually gone swimming in the Nile, so I'm quite glad there aren't still crocodiles bobbing around in there . . .

WHERE DID ALL THE METAL GO?

It's also possible that this incredible crocodile armour in our treasure chest was made during a time when the Romans could not source enough metal to make metal armour. We know about this time because of the writing of an ancient Roman called Vegetius. He is quite a mysterious character – in the fourth century CE he wrote two books: one about war and one about being a vet!

Vegetius was horrified when the Romans began running low on metal because they'd dug so much out of the mines they controlled. He thought that because the Roman Empire couldn't afford proper equipment anymore (like the kit they had in the glory days one or two centuries before) it meant they were becoming weak. This lack of metal armour almost certainly meant Roman soldiers were more likely to be wounded and killed in battle. And not everyone could have afforded or would have been able to find armour made out of crocodile skin. It must have been a scary time for Roman soldiers. Imagine sending a loved one off to fight in a battle knowing he hadn't been given proper armour to wear?

Before metal ran low, the Romans had invented several types of armour. One of their favourites was chainmail, which was made by linking thousands of tiny metal loops together to form a material that's basically rows and rows of chain – very similar to what medieval knights wore. The Romans also liked to mould, carve or paint muscles on their armour plates, as it made them look even stronger and scarier to their opponents, so they'd also sometimes give themselves a **fake six-pack!** Romans sometimes even gave their horses armour!

Just have one more feel of that crocodile suit – it's not every day you get to stroke a crocodile's skin, is it? I'm not surprised this was buried as treasure – it really is just so special.

Hang on a second, what's this –

HUGE teeth?

Look how sharp these ones are! That's because they belonged to...

a dragon!

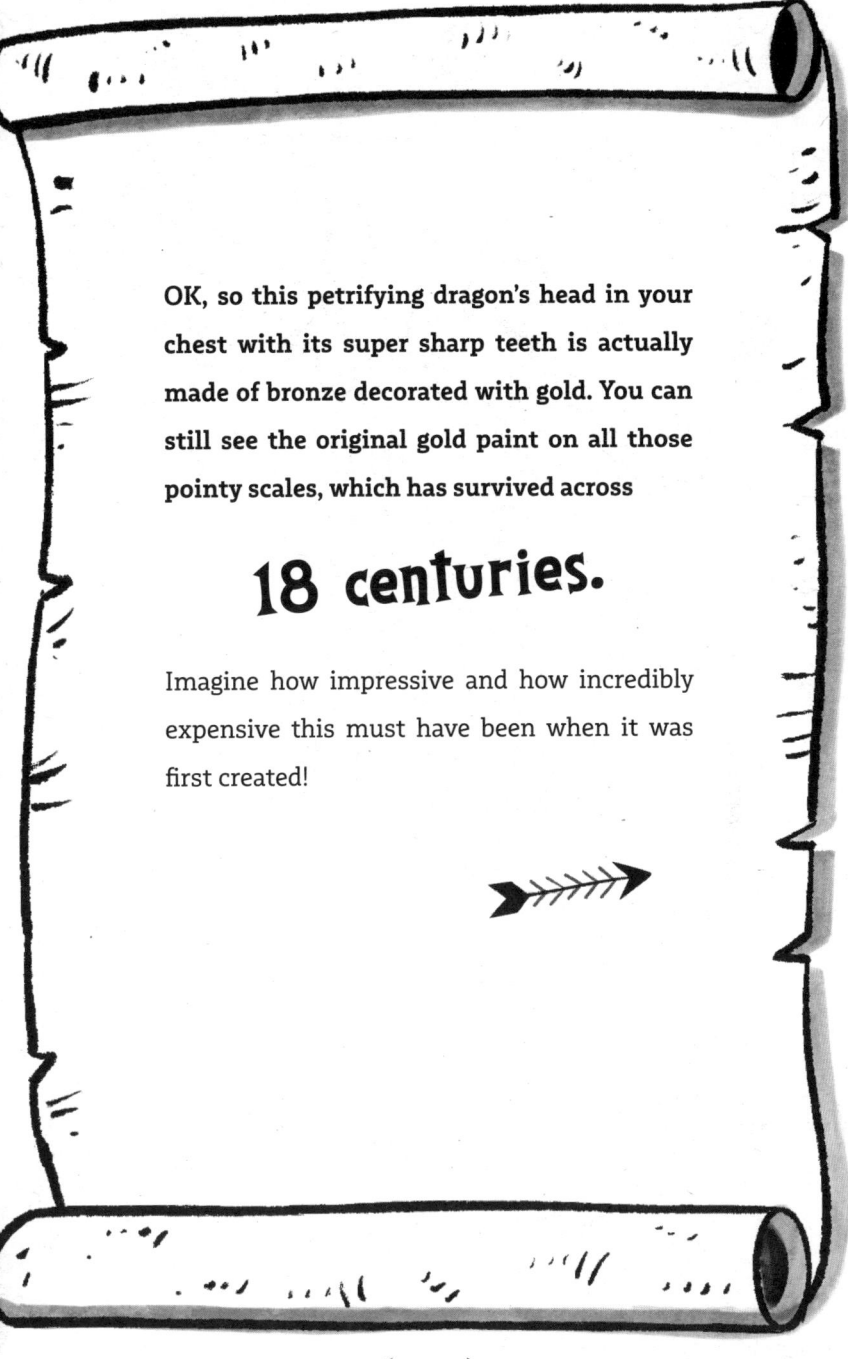

OK, so this petrifying dragon's head in your chest with its super sharp teeth is actually made of bronze decorated with gold. You can still see the original gold paint on all those pointy scales, which has survived across

18 centuries.

Imagine how impressive and how incredibly expensive this must have been when it was first created!

BEWARE OF THE DRAGON

That dragon's head is only a tiny bit of the monster. Behind it is a billowing windsock (a fabric tube that catches the air, fills out and ripples when you run along with it). And it probably would've been painted in bright colours. The effect of the bronze head and windsock together would have made it look like a dragon was dashing along the road, and Roman soldiers would have carried it into battle to intimidate their enemies.

Before the Roman army started using them, these dragons were used by the Sarmatians – a people from the country we now call Iran. Sarmatians were excellent horsemen. They settled in the lands between the Caspian and Black Seas around the second century BCE – so just at the time Rome was rising to power. I've been to that area myself and have seen super-skilled horsemen still riding around in the mountains, sometimes with foals galloping along behind them.

These amazing riders today often don't have fixed homes. Instead they camp, rise at dawn, travel to a new spot, and camp again.

I also found a burial of Roman soldiers there. This shows us that ancient Romans made it that far east too; they reached as far as the place now called Azerbaijan, located between Russia and the Caspian Sea.

The Romans were so inspired by the Sarmatians that they adopted their idea of dragon banners and marched into battle brandishing them as the soldiers advanced. This solid bronze head measures 18 x 30 centimetres and Romans would've held it up with a two-metre-long pole. Then they had to run fast enough to make it look like a living dragon was racing along beside them. This would have required enormous strength and the ability to dodge obstacles, fast.

And it must have looked **awesome!**

To add to the effect, when the wind travelled into the dragon's gaping mouth, it would have made a hissing, whistling sound.

The Romans certainly liked to add a bit of theatre to their battles, didn't they?

Did you know that many Romans thought dragons were real? They even added dragons to their maps. They believed dragons really lived in the most remote and wild places. For instance, the Romans thought that Britain (which they called Britannia), must be inhabited by dragons because the whole of the UK back then was so wild, rough and barbaric.

Dig deeper into the chest and you'll see something that looks like a massive roll of wallpaper. But that can't be right, so what is it?

It's actually a map – it's 35 centimetres high and nearly seven metres long!

I wonder where it's going to lead us?

Maybe it's a treasure map in a treasure chest!

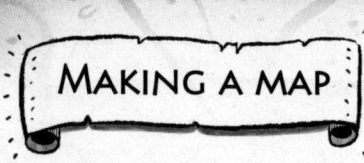

MAKING A MAP

I adore hand-drawn maps like this. They must have been so much fun to make. Before there were aeroplanes, helicopters or drones, mapmakers had to imagine looking down on planet Earth with what's called a bird's-eye view. They also had to make real, dangerous and difficult journeys on the ground, and then decide what were the most interesting and important things to include on their chart. In Roman times, map-makers were often soldiers, because they were the ones who got to travel far beyond the borders of the city of Rome and visit places that were new to them. So they were the best-placed people to show others what the rest of the world looked like.

Ancient maps were carried around as a practical, working guide to a place (there were no satnavs back then!) and so were often made of waterproof parchment. (Parchment is a kind of writing material made of the stretched-out skin of an animal, usually a goat.) This made them easy to roll up and handy for soldiers who regularly marched about 50 kilometres a day in all weathers on campaign to conquer new territories or stop rebellions in their conquered lands. The soldiers often got very soggy, but at least their maps could be wiped down and didn't disintegrate in the rain!

Parchment is believed to have been named for the ancient city of **Pergamon** (which is in modern-day Turkey). Pergamon had a hospital, which, because it was built around 2,300 years ago, makes it one of the oldest hospitals in history. In fact, there was a famous medical pioneer called Galen who worked in Pergamon – and one of the reasons he got so much practice was because he was able to try out his medical skills on wounded gladiators from the gladiator school that was also there. Citizens of Pergamon cared a lot about mental health as well as physical health. When people were having a tough time or were feeling down, they tried treating them with joyful things like sunbathing, musical performances and water therapy – listening to the sound of running water, bathing in spring water and having lovely massages next to ponds – as well as with more traditional medicine.

WHERE DOES THIS MAP TAKE US?

This giant map in your treasure chest shows the detail of the entire Roman Empire! It includes roads built by soldiers, their military camps, the Nile and the many cities the empire covered.

PERGAMON

You can see Pergamon on the map. It is south-east of a city called Byzantium, which the Emperor Constantine (272–337 CE) renamed Constantinople after himself, when it became the new capital of the Roman Empire. Constantinople is now called Istanbul by most people, and it is the largest city in Turkey.

Pompeii and Herculaneum are also on the map. This is really interesting. Their presence on the map is a clue – a bit like in a historical detective story! They suggest that Rome's first emperor, Augustus, commissioned the original version of this map before Pompeii and Herculaneum were destroyed by that awful eruption of Mount Vesuvius.

POMPEII

Head west along the map and you'll see the town of Kukes. Kukes was located in what we now call Albania. In ancient times it was a much larger territory owned by a powerful tribe known as the Illyrians; the Romans called the whole region Illyria after the tribe.

There is a road running from the edge of the sea next to Italy up to what's now Istanbul, through Albania, Northern Macedonia, Greece and Turkey, which was called the Egnatian Way (or the *Via Egnatia*, as they would have said in Latin).

> Grab a piece of paper and a pencil and try drawing your own map! Then you'll be travelling along ancient Roman roads like soldiers, or following in the footsteps of children who moved across the Roman Empire, maybe even the child who gathered up all these fascinating treasures and left this treasure chest behind for us to find . . .

ROME

If you zoom in to the city of Constantinople, or New Rome, itself, you can see Venus, the goddess of love, looking after the city. I think Venus was chosen as Rome's protector, because like all cities, it was a complicated place, with many people, all with different ideas about life and how to live and all trying to get along together. So they needed a lot of love to help them stick together and not be rowing the whole time! That's why people back then thought Venus was the best goddess to be a patron of their cities. (A 'patron' is similar to a fairy godmother – a kind, caring and protective presence to support you. In ancient Rome, there were whole systems of 'patronage' where a 'patron' would provide protection for someone in return for that person's loyalty.)

THE ROMAN ROADS

Pretty much the whole Roman road system is represented on this remarkable parchment, and it shows just how far the Romans expanded their vast empire. You can even see

Roman ports all the way over towards India. That's why the map is so big – to fit it all in!

Roman roads were a key part of the Roman Empire's success. They connected all the major towns and cities in the empire. Often dead straight, these roads were built up on layers of gravel and sand, and sometimes had paving slabs laid on top. Roman soldiers built them and had special privileges to walk along them, while traders and ordinary travellers were only allowed on these roads if there were no soldiers in sight.

The roles of Roman soldiers went far beyond just fighting (just think about all those maps they were making, for instance!). The Emperor Trajan (53–117 CE) built a monumental column (Trajan's Column, completed in 113 CE) in Rome to celebrate his military victories. However, there are not as many carvings of the battles on the column, as you might expect. Instead, there are scenes that show Roman soldiers marching in orderly lines and clearing land for new roads. The emperor knew that without roads he couldn't keep control of his empire – so that's why he celebrated street-building on this expensive, high-profile work of art.

All along Roman roads – particularly when later rulers

like Emperor Trajan and Emperor Hadrian (76–138 CE) were in charge – you would also have found milestones, which were stones marked with distances. They were placed mile after mile so soldiers could see how long they'd been marching for, and how far it was to the next fort or camp. And yes, soldiers would have built those forts and camps too. They were definitely kept busy! (They must all have been very fit and battle-ready.)

> Some soldiers had maps painted on to their shields. I don't know whether that was to help them find their way or just to prove how well travelled they were. I think it was probably so they could show off to the other armies they came up against about how vast their empire was.

There's a stone version of this particular map in the middle of Rome, next to the Altar of Peace (see page 31). Being shown how far their empire spread must have made even the most ordinary Roman citizen feel as if they owned

the whole world!

We can all draw maps if we want to – and they can feature anything you want! We can choose to include things that are most important to us. Personally, I'd put all the places where the coolest and most unique types of cats live!

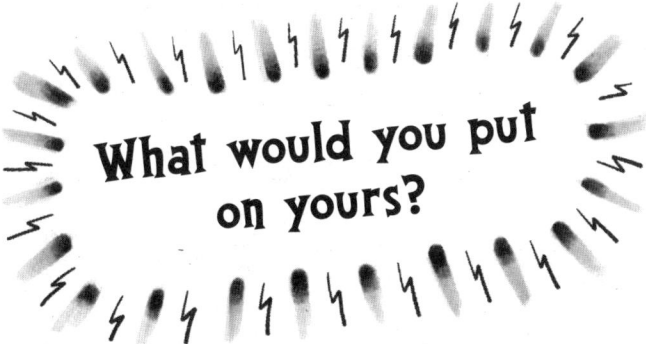

Roll the map up and pop it back into the chest. You might need to peer more closely to find the next object, which is

much,

much

smaller than the map.

This piece of treasure is tiny, isn't it? Tiny, but gorgeous. A bit of treasure that looks and feels like just the kind of thing a pirate would have had in their treasure chest. In fact, this jewel, shining like a ruby, might actually have come from a real pirate's hoard!

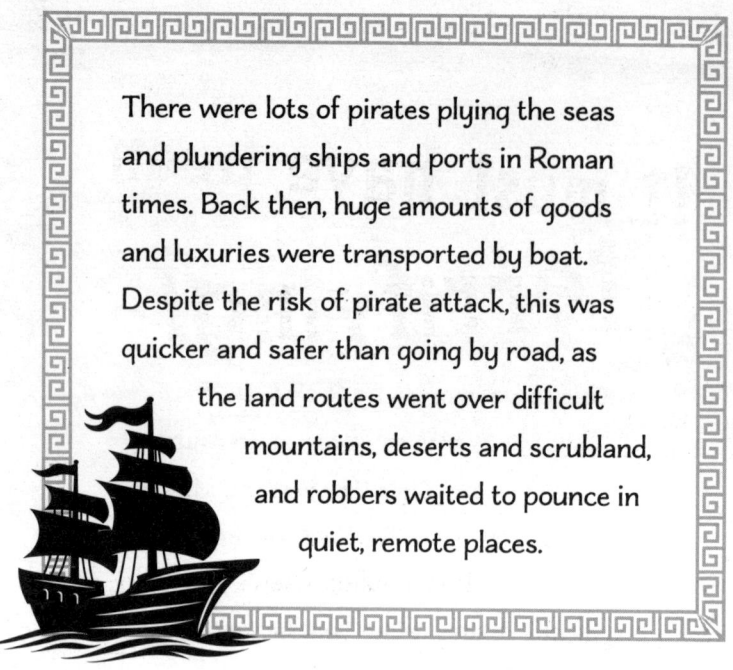

There were lots of pirates plying the seas and plundering ships and ports in Roman times. Back then, huge amounts of goods and luxuries were transported by boat. Despite the risk of pirate attack, this was quicker and safer than going by road, as the land routes went over difficult mountains, deserts and scrubland, and robbers waited to pounce in quiet, remote places.

Boats would be packed with valuable and useful things. But the boats weren't always safe options either. There were lots of people on board, and seaborne thieves were tempted by the possibility of capturing and enslaving sailors and travellers and merchants. In fact, it was Rome's constant demand for slaves that encouraged some pirates. They would lie in wait in little coves and then race out on unsuspecting ships, jump on board and grab all the people to sell into slavery at slave markets like the one in Delos that I mentioned earlier. Can you imagine it?

It must have been terrifying!

The famous Roman leader Julius Caesar was once even taken hostage by pirates. Mind you, he wreaked a terrible revenge – after he was released, Julius Caesar made sure the pirates who had taken him captive were caught and crucified.

The Romans prided themselves on how good they were at chasing pirates off. They even had a special anti-pirate fleet! They persuaded some people living in what are now Turkey and Greece to let them take control of their land, in return for dealing with the scourge of pirates on the Mediterranean. And one Roman general, Pompey, persuaded a certain bunch of pirates to give up their piratical ways and settle down to become farmers instead.

A GLOWING GARNET

That glistening gemstone in your hand is called a garnet, a stone that usually comes from the countries now called India and Sri Lanka. So that little gem must have travelled thousands of miles to get to Rome, and now it's travelled even further to end up in your back garden!

The Romans thought garnets were beautiful – and a bit magical because they glowed like burning coals. Romans would set them in earrings, belts and necklaces; they even used them to decorate tack ('tack' is the collective term for horse-riding equipment – the bridle, saddle and reins) to make their horses look splendid. They also used garnets as decorations because they believed these red-glowing stones might help ward off demons – so they were highly treasured items!

The word garnet, by the way, comes from the word pomegranate – a fruit that grows very happily in places such as Greece, Italy and Turkey. Pomegranates are bright red, like that precious gemstone.

> How much do you think this garnet would be worth now? Well, it would probably sell for around £5,000. You could buy a plane ticket to fly all around the world with that amount. Only a very wealthy family would have been able to afford to buy a gem that was so costly.

TRADING WITH INDIA

Globalization is the word we use to describe the way countries across the world connect, communicate and trade with one another. Globalization isn't a modern thing – we know that people in ancient societies travelled and made connections with others many thousands of miles away, on whole other continents.

It was Emperor Augustus who became especially determined to trade with people in India. Romans loved Indian spices, as well as pearls, garnets and other jewels that were found there. Luckily, Indian kings and traders absolutely LOVED Roman wine, so trade deals were easily agreed.

It must have been such an adventure, setting out to sea in a sailing ship to cross the oceans with your ship's hull loaded with precious goods from India, heading back to Europe. It was the 'trade winds' blowing around the Indian Ocean that allowed this to happen. These are winds that put huge amounts of energy into a boat's sails. They are also sometimes called 'easterlies' because they always blow from east to west, so they helped to power the ships coming to Rome from places like India . . . as long as you were able to avoid those pesky pirates!

We're lucky to have photos and videos, so we actually know what people and places across the world look like . . . and not just listen to rumours and fantasies about other lands. The author and traveller Pliny the Elder (who we learned about on page 18) held many false beliefs about India and the people who lived there. He actually thought there was a tribe of one-legged people called Monopods, who hopped about and used their single giant foot like an umbrella when they needed to shelter from the sun. Pliny was obviously just listening to terrible, fake travellers' tales. But the idea caught on in Rome and some Romans really believed in the Monopods.

Wow.

As well as precious stones and other goods, Romans transported animals. Horses in particular were moved about, sometimes in special boats that were adapted to keep the horses inside safe and secure, and were carried to far-flung places for use by the military. Clearly, then, horses were considered valuable – but special enough to have their own jewellery?

Let's take a closer look at the next object to find out more.

The Romans **loved** horses and dogs, although, unlike ancient Egyptians, they weren't that keen on cats. For some reason, they seemed to think cats couldn't always be trusted. There aren't many mentions of cats in literature, or evidence of cat names or pictures of them in Roman houses.

How can you **not** be keen on cats? They're so clever and cool!

I think it's why I prefer the Greeks to the Romans – because the ancient Greeks were more cat people! Anyway, whatever their views on cats, the Romans loved horses, so you might not be too surprised to discover the next shiny thing in the chest. It looks like a piece of jewellery, doesn't it? But it's not meant for humans . . . this fabulous treasure is jewellery for a horse!

HAVE YOU EVER SEEN A HORSE WEARING EARRINGS?

The child who so carefully stored all these precious goods away in this chest would have often seen horses dressed in shining jewellery. This could have been during religious ceremonies, or if they ever caught a glimpse of the emperor and his personal bodyguard, the Imperial Guard or Praetorian Guard (created by the first official Roman emperor, Augustus), parading through the streets of Rome. Whoever owned this beautiful jewellery would have draped it around the horse's chest.

There are bits that look like earrings, which are pendants, and would have dangled and jangled around the horse's head. Pendants came in all sorts of shapes and forms, including leaves, hearts, teardrops and crescent moons.

One of the reasons why the Romans (and many people before them) carefully arranged jewellery (and sometimes bells) like this around their horses' heads was to create a comforting, regular noise for the horses to hear. This was intended to distract them from the disturbing cacophony of either busy streets and merchants shouting about sewage drains overflowing, or battle noises like the blast of a soldier's trumpet used to order armies into combat.

Smelly!

THE MANY USES OF HORSES

Horses were invaluable to the Romans and were traded all around the empire. Many came from Spain and North Africa. They often had to cross the Mediterranean to Rome by sea, which must have been really difficult to organize logistically, and horrible for the horses – animals are usually terrified of going in boats, even ones that have been specially adapted.

Horses helped the Romans with many aspects of their lives, including carrying soldiers into battle (remember that horse armour we mentioned before, on page 141?) and hauling supplies from one town to another. (Other strong animals were used to shift cargo too, such as donkeys, mules, oxen, water buffalo and even elephants!) Fast horses were also a vital part of the postal service, carrying couriers and their messages all over the empire and beyond.

However, the horses decked out in all that fabulous bronze, gold and silver jewellery probably weren't meant to be ridden by a single person; they were most likely used to pull a chariot.

The Romans were very keen on chariots, as you know, and they used them a lot in warfare. Soldiers looked pretty imposing charging across a battlefield on the back of a chariot, and they could also make a hasty retreat if the fighting turned against them.

Romans loved to race for fun in chariots too. On this piece of jewellery is a fleck of red paint – which was probably the colour of the chariot team that this horse was pulling. Successful chariot racing teams could become really, really popular in ancient Rome, with their own passionate fan bases who followed their results and cheered them on when they competed. Sometimes chariot-race fans even fought with the fans of rival teams! Basically, chariot racing in ancient Rome was the equivalent of our football leagues today. The most popular Roman chariot teams were called the Reds, the Whites, the Blues and the Greens. The really swanky teams – the Purples and the Golds – were created by the Emperor Domitian (51–96 CE) and had the best trainers, the most expensive equipment and the poshest digs to stay in. The Purples and the Golds were like the number-one seeds at the Wimbledon tennis championship, so they didn't race all the time – only at really important games. (Mind you, they vanish from the records after the Emperor Domitian died, so maybe they were just too expensive to maintain and came to be thought of as a mad-capped idea of just one emperor.)

Lots of supporters bet money on which chariot team they thought would win. You can lose a lot of money by betting, and there were many cases of Romans going bankrupt and losing everything as a result of bad gambles.

CHARIOT RACING

Chariot racing was a very dangerous sport. Charioteers often carried daggers, so if they crashed, they could cut themselves free of any reins or bridles they got caught up in, to avoid getting accidentally run over by their rivals. But that also meant that when they crashed, they sometimes got stabbed with their own weapons.

OUCH!

However, winning charioteers (who, like gladiators, were often enslaved people) could sometimes earn enough money to buy their freedom. We know from Roman authors at the time that at least one charioteer earned 60,000 *sesterces* (a *sestertius* was a coin worth a quarter of a *denarius*) for just one race – that's around £30,000 in today's money!

Horses that did well in the races became famous too, and we still know some of their names: Pompeianus, Lucidus, Galata.

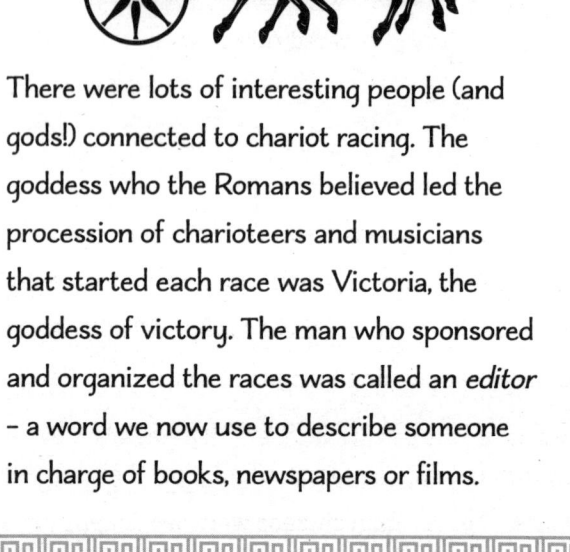

There were lots of interesting people (and gods!) connected to chariot racing. The goddess who the Romans believed led the procession of charioteers and musicians that started each race was Victoria, the goddess of victory. The man who sponsored and organized the races was called an *editor* – a word we now use to describe someone in charge of books, newspapers or films.

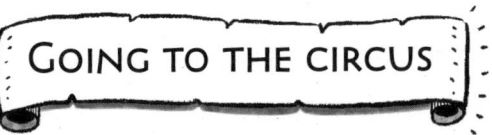

Going to the circus

To us, a circus is a big round tent full of performers and acrobats, but in Rome a *circus* was an open circuit where chariot races took place. The most famous was the Circus Maximus, which you've heard about (see page 89). It's still there in Rome, and you can visit and walk around it (or run around pretending you're in a chariot race!) – although it's a grass-covered ruin now.

If you were a poor person in Rome, or someone called a 'pleb' ('pleb' is short for the Roman word *plebian*), you were allowed to go to the *circus* for free. Wealthy people got seats under an awning that protected them from the sun. Because of this (and because Roman emperors handed out bread to people who couldn't afford it for themselves), there is a phrase that Roman citizens were kept happy (or at least kept quiet) because they were given 'bread and circuses' to satisfy them.

Children were not allowed into the Circus Maximus to watch chariot races, or the Colosseum to watch gladiator fights. However, on rare occasions there might have been children in the arena itself. While fights were traditionally between adult men and were horrible enough, the Emperor Nero (37–68 CE) organized fights that used both female and child gladiators.

So, that dignified decoration you're holding – so heavy because it's made of silver and semi-precious stones, and worth more than a real pony would cost today – will almost certainly at one time have been lurching and crashing and jangling around the neck of a prized chariot-race horse.

Just imagine the roar of the crowd as it sped around one of ancient Rome's huge stadiums dedicated to entertaining its people.

Do you know what? I think we've saved the best until last! Look at that tile at the very bottom of the chest.

It's an old roof tile made from terracotta, a type of hardened clay. (Remember, the word 'terracotta' comes from *terra*, which is Latin for earth, and *cotta*, which means cooked.) It was a very common building material for both rooves and floors in ancient Rome, so there are a lot of terracotta tiles about.

CREEPING CATS

It looks like there's a paw print on the tile! What kind of animal do you reckon it belonged to? A small dog? A cat? A paw print is an odd decoration to put on a roof tile, isn't it? Perhaps it wasn't a decoration at all. Perhaps a cat walked across the soft clay tile after it had been left out to dry in the sun!

Typical cats . . . how naughty!

It's very hard to train cats - they live by their own rules! However, we know some Romans tried to train them to do certain things. There's an interesting picture carved into a piece of stone that shows a Roman attempting to train a cat to climb up a ladder, and another cat being trained to walk on its hind legs by having a bird dangled above its head!

The cat that left that perfect paw print on the tile was probably a stray cat. In fact, there were so many strays in Rome at one time that it became known as the 'city of cats'. All these cats were probably tempted in because Rome was infested with mice and rats, which loved all the waste and rubbish left behind by the million or so people who lived there. (Rubbish wasn't collected like it is now, so there was always lots of old food and waste lying around on the streets.) Cats would have been lured in by the smell of all those rodents. The original cats would then have had kittens, who became the famous cat inhabitants of Rome. As a result, the cats of Rome were excellent pest-controllers that mostly lived outdoors.

BEWARE OF THE DOG!

Lots of Romans actually liked to keep weasels as pets, especially because they ate mice, beetles and other creepy-crawlies. And some Roman families had pet pigs. We know of one pet pig that escaped on to the Egnatian Way (that long Roman road I mentioned on page 155) and then got run over. The owner was so upset he put up a memorial to his pig friend on the roadside. (If you want to visit that pig-praising headstone, it's now in a museum in Edessa in Northern Macedonia.)

But one of the Romans' favourite animals was the dog, as a pet and as a working animal. In fact, they adored dogs so much they engraved pictures of them on golden bracelets and silver cups.

There's a famous mosaic from a house entrance in Pompeii that shows a ferocious dog. Underneath it says *CAVE CANEM*, which means **BEWARE OF THE DOG!** – sometimes you still see this warning on people's back gates today. I wonder if the mosaic might have been used to show off, almost as if to say

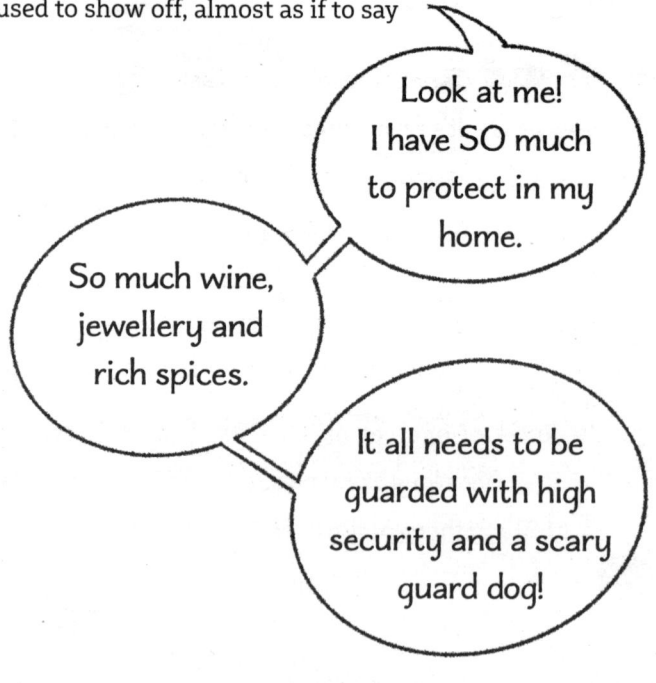

Look at me! I have SO much to protect in my home.

So much wine, jewellery and rich spices.

It all needs to be guarded with high security and a scary guard dog!

We know that Romans believed evil spirits were all around them, so they may have believed the *Cave Canem* dog protected their home from demons, too.

The *Cave Canem* mosaic is fantastically well made. It's probably composed of about 100,000 little coloured stone cubes. A wonderful detail you can see if you look closely is the red bits placed in the guard dog's eyes to make it look even fiercer. The dog wears a bejewelled collar; such lavish decorations were another way of showing other people and guests how rich you were.

The breed of dog shown in the *Cave Canem* mosaic was fearsome indeed! It was a massive breed called the Molossian hound, which looked like a cross between a Great Dane and a Saluki. They are now extinct, but their descendants are called Neapolitan mastiffs. Weighing up to 70 kilograms (which is about the weight of 14 cats) and standing around three-quarters of a metre tall, Neapolitan mastiffs are very large and very impressive animals!

The household hounds needed to be strong because they weren't just guard dogs, they were also hunting dogs. Romans (and Greeks, and lots of other ancient civilizations) loved hunting, and there were several reasons for this. It provided meat to eat; chasing and killing wild animals showed everyone in your town or village how brave you were; and hunting animals such as boar and deer kept their populations under control and reduced the likelihood of them wandering into the cities from the wilds and eating people's crops.

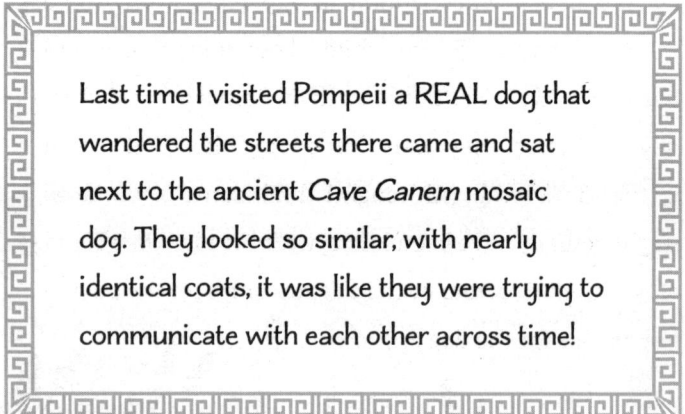

Last time I visited Pompeii a REAL dog that wandered the streets there came and sat next to the ancient *Cave Canem* mosaic dog. They looked so similar, with nearly identical coats, it was like they were trying to communicate with each other across time!

Part of the Family

We know of one young Roman who really loved their family dog because they carved a picture of it on to their tombstone. Actually, Roman children were often depicted on their own tombstones with animals: cats, hares, roosters, geese and sometimes butterflies! 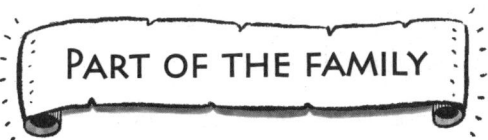 This shows that Roman children were sometimes encouraged to be animal lovers. (Which is good; I believe passionately that loving animals around us is such a rewarding and nourishing thing to be able to do!)

Another Roman tombstone features a dog called Pearl. The Latin inscription tells us that Pearl was kind and gentle and used to curl up on the end of her owner's bed every night. I think Pearl must have been greatly loved, don't you?

And here's a description of a pet dog from some Roman writing: 'Foster-child, soul-companion and deserving of praise.' Some ancient Romans loved their dogs so much they were buried together with them in the same tomb. (Although I think some of the dogs might actually have been killed, with the idea they could stay with their owner even in death – nice for the owner, not so nice for the dog . . .)

Another ancient tile, just like the one in your chest, has been found with a dog's paw print on it. Perhaps animals liked walking over unfinished wet clay rooves because the clay felt cool against the pads of their feet; after all, it was probably a boiling-hot day, otherwise tiles wouldn't have been laid out in the sun to dry in the first place!

This is why finding treasures like this is so fascinating – it helps us think like problem-solvers – piecing bits of the jigsaw puzzle of the past together.

Even unexpected little fragments of evidence like this tell us a lot about ancient life . . . and the lives of children just like you, who lived in the Roman world around 2,000 years ago.

JUST IMAGINE:
if you'd lived in ancient Rome, you could even have had a pet weasel!

Well, we've examined everything in the chest now. Perhaps we should put it all back, close the lid and rebury it so someone else in the future can find, enjoy and learn from the treasure hoard, too.

But before we do that, let's just think for a moment longer about all these fascinating treasures, and the ancient secrets and clues to the past they've given us. Every single one was a beloved object that once belonged to a person; all the treasures have their own tales to tell and teach us so much about life in ancient Rome. By rediscovering them and their stories, we've been able to think about history, and about the people who lived in it.

I'm glad that the chest didn't get lost forever. And I hope the child who packed it up so carefully is pleased that we've found it at the bottom of your garden, opened it up and learned about their world from all those years ago.

It's a horrible feeling losing something precious, isn't it? And yet I believe that even if something has been lost, someone out there will one day find it, and treasure it as much as I did. Treasuring gifts from the past is one of the ways we can connect with people across thousands of miles and thousands of years.

So if you ever go exploring in fields or parks yourself, do look out for unusual bits and pieces in the earth or the sand that might have been dropped by someone who lived before you. Because the brilliant truth is that unless something from the past has been destroyed, it is lying there somewhere, just waiting to be found by someone like you!

And if you ever find any ancient treasures – however great or small – take a picture of them, leave everything where you spotted it, and tell someone from a museum about what you've discovered. (You'll need to ask a grown-up to help you with this straight away, because there are all sorts of rules about treasure and how and when to tell someone about it. For example, it needs to be reported within 14 days of finding it if you live in the United Kingdom. Ask an adult to look up 'Treasure Act 1996' on the internet to find out more.) And of course if you ever find a whole treasure chest, as well as the official people who need to know, please contact me too! I'd be so excited!

What an adventure this chest has taken us on ... we've learned about animals both real and imaginary, about the rich and the poor in the Roman world, the enslaved and the free, about music and food and magic and jewels and soldiers and homes – and a lot about the wider Roman world too. It's allowed us to use our imaginations to travel back in time, and has left me feeling inspired. I hope you feel the same!

The Romans ruled people who lived in three continents (Europe, Asia and Africa) for around 600 years.

The lives and experiences of both the rulers and the ruled matter because they helped to create the world we live in today.

And do you know what the best thing about all this is? There could be more chests just waiting to be discovered and unpacked! Wouldn't it be wonderful if we could find another one from a different time?

A box full of jewellery and armour from the Viking age, perhaps. Or a chest of statuettes and mummies from ancient Egypt?

Let's keep our fingers crossed and hope that happens very soon . . .

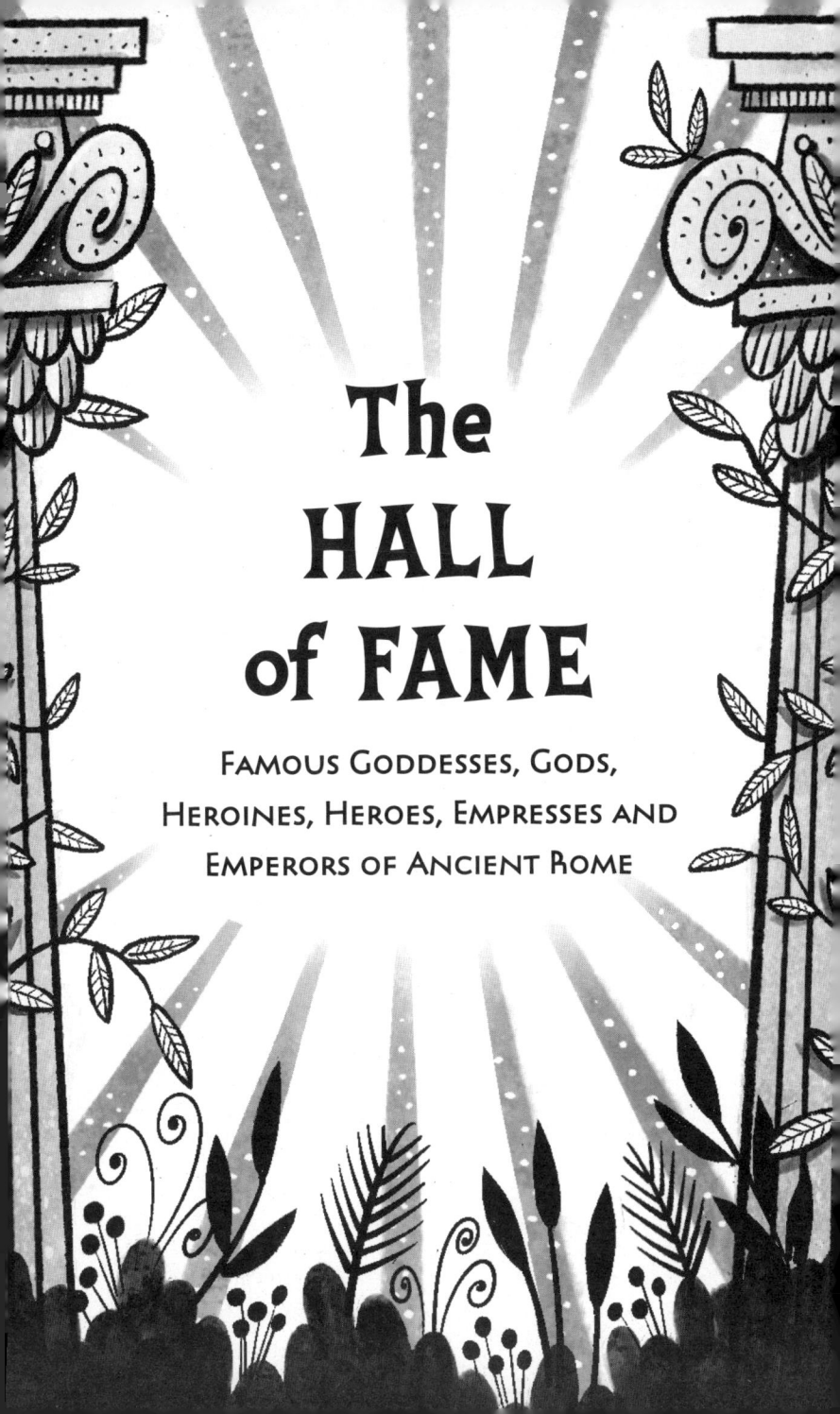

The HALL of FAME

FAMOUS GODDESSES, GODS, HEROINES, HEROES, EMPRESSES AND EMPERORS OF ANCIENT ROME

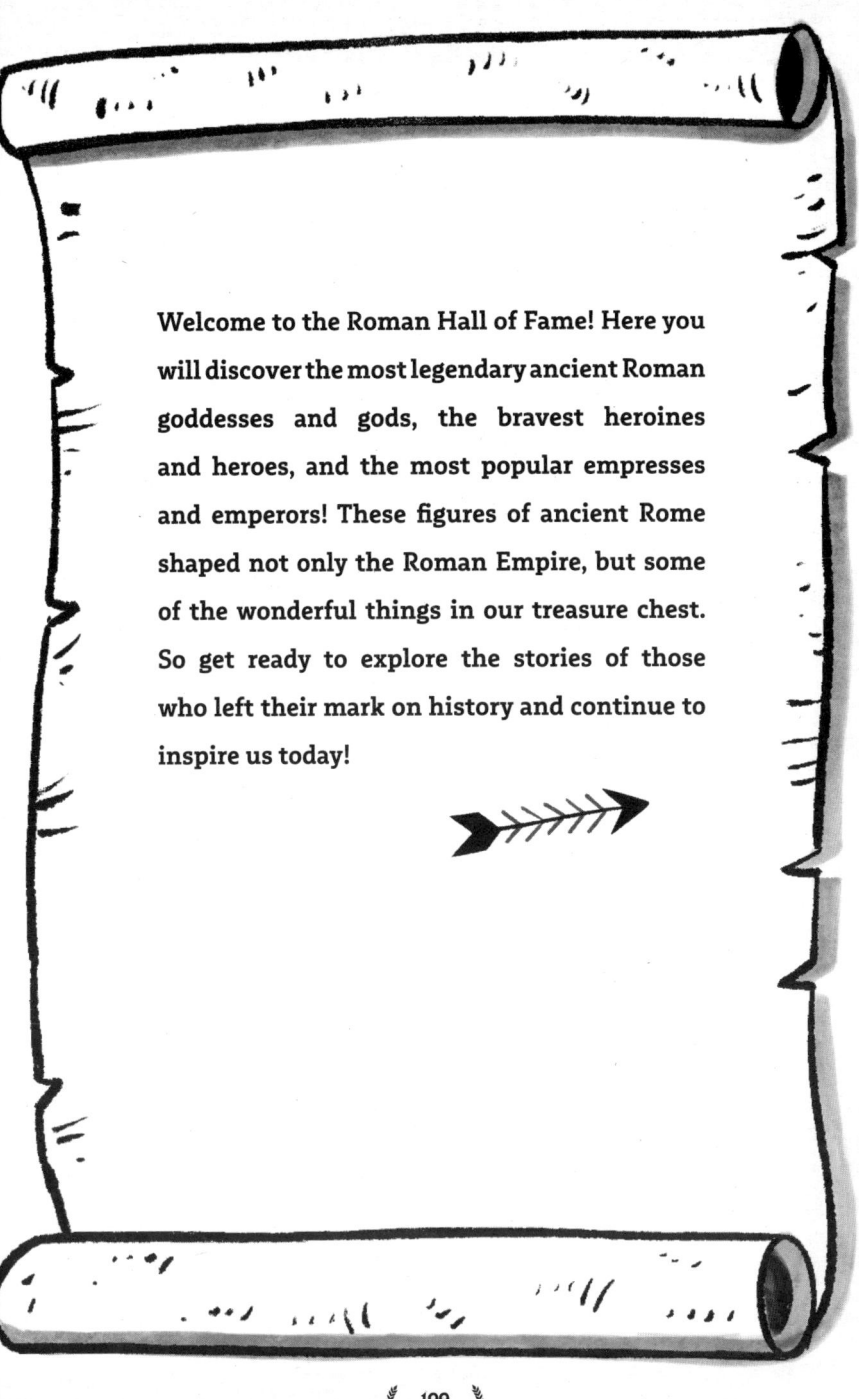

Welcome to the Roman Hall of Fame! Here you will discover the most legendary ancient Roman goddesses and gods, the bravest heroines and heroes, and the most popular empresses and emperors! These figures of ancient Rome shaped not only the Roman Empire, but some of the wonderful things in our treasure chest. So get ready to explore the stories of those who left their mark on history and continue to inspire us today!

Goddesses and Gods of Roman Mythology

Diana

Diana (or Artemis to the Greeks), the Roman goddess of hunting, was fierce and fearless, and inspired young girls with her bravery. She is often shown with a bow and her loyal hunting dog or bird of prey by her side. She also represented the moon (her twin brother, Apollo, represented the sun) and she watched over women during childbirth, giving them strength and balance in their lives. Diana was also linked to the underworld (where the Romans believed people went after they died), helping lost souls find their way.

Minerva

In Greek mythology she is known as Athena, but to the Romans, she is Minerva – the wise goddess of warfare, justice and victory. Born fully armoured and springing directly from the head of the king of the gods, Jupiter, Minerva embodied both strength and intelligence, often accompanied by her sacred owl, a symbol of wisdom. Unlike her unpredictable brother, Mars, Minerva preferred a clever approach to conflict, but beware – she had a quick temper and held grudges against those who dared to offend her!

Fortuna

Fortuna, whose name means fortune, was a fascinating goddess who symbolized both good and bad luck! As the daughter of Jupiter, she had incredible power, blessing women with the ability to have children and influencing the outcome of battles. This made her a very important goddess in the everyday lives of Romans as the empire grew in the first and second centuries CE. She is often depicted sitting on a ball and holding a rudder to remind us of destiny's twists and turns and to guide us through challenges, and she is usually holding a horn called a cornucopia overflowing with riches. Fortuna was celebrated throughout Italy. So the next time you experience a stroke of luck or an unexpected turn of events, remember that she may just be at work!

Proserpina

Proserpina, the enchanting queen of the underworld, captivated the hearts of many as she ruled alongside her husband, Pluto (Hades to the Greeks), the lord of the dead. Also known as Persephone, she was both the vibrant goddess of spring, embodying life's cycle, and also responsible for guiding souls to their fates in the afterlife. With her striking golden and dark hair, she bridged the worlds of the living and the dead, light and dark, taking care of the earth and ensuring that harvests flourished.

Venus

Venus (also known as Aphrodite), the enchanting goddess of love and beauty, was believed to have been born from the frothy waves of the sea. She held the hearts of mortals (regular human beings) in her delicate hands, proving that love truly conquers all! While Venus inspired desire and prosperity, she also symbolized Rome's power, and could be ferocious if anyone dared to compare themselves to her or compete with her. Often depicted with blooming roses and myrtle, she was a guardian of nature and people's hearts, and the proud mother of Cupid, whose arrows of love made sure that no one could escape her influence!

Apollo

Apollo, the radiant twin brother of Diana, was celebrated as the god of the sun, healing, music and prophecy, and was believed to race a golden chariot across the sky at sunrise and sunset. The Romans honoured him not only for his ability to unleash plagues on the wicked but also for his role as a compassionate healer. They worshipped him to avoid misfortune. With a dazzling bow that twinkled like a star and embodied power, and a lyre that filled the air with delightful melodies, Apollo became a cherished role model for young men across the Roman Empire!

Jupiter – the father of the gods!

Jupiter, the king of the Roman gods (called Zeus by the Greeks), was the most powerful and feared of all, often represented by an eagle to symbolize Roman victory. He ruled over the sky, thunder and lightning – so when you hear a storm, it could be Jupiter showing his power! Jupiter also protected Rome by building relationships and making agreements with other people and places. He would often visit people in disguise to test their hospitality, known as *hospitium*, inspiring the Roman custom of offering food, shelter and kindness to strangers in one's home.

Juno

Juno (called Hera by the Greeks), the queen of the gods, and wife of Jupiter, the king of the gods, was a strong and protective goddess, especially when it came to women, marriage and family. She was also a guardian in times of war and played an important role in Roman society, with many temples built especially for girls and women to ask for her protection. Juno was often linked with symbols like the peacock and pomegranate, representing her power, beauty and her role as a fierce and caring mother figure.

Vulcan

As the god of fire, forge and metalwork, Vulcan (or Hephaestus to the Greeks) was the creative genius behind Jupiter's thunderbolts and Minerva's powerful spears, which showcased his unmatched metalworking skills. Despite being thrown off Mount Olympus by Juno as a baby, he transformed his struggles into strength, proving himself to be a hardworking and resilient deity of the Roman Pantheon. Symbolizing both the awe-inspiring power and unpredictable nature of fire, he worked alongside humans to ensure the survival of the empire, earning respect through his brilliant creations and tireless dedication!

Mars

Mars (also known as Ares), the fearsome god of war, was someone you didn't want to face on the battlefield; his love for violence made him a valuable ally for armies seeking victory! With his mighty shield and his symbols of intimidating vultures and dogs, he protected cities from invasion and symbolized military power. However, Mars also played a vital role in protecting land, farms and crops during wartime and had a softer side as a loving partner to Venus and the proud father of legendary figures like Romulus, Remus and Cupid.

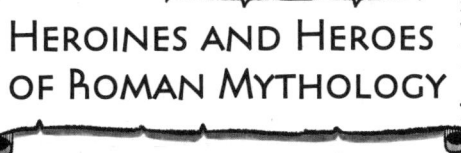

Heroines and Heroes of Roman Mythology

Cloelia

Cloelia, our first Roman heroine, became a bit of a superhero when she was offered as a hostage in exchange for peace between the Romans and Etruscans in 508 BCE. She planned an escape from the Etruscans, leading other hostages to safety by swimming across the Tiber River to return to Rome. In recognition of her daring act, the Etruscan king granted her and other hostages their freedom while the Romans honoured her with a statue on horseback – something almost unheard of for a woman in ancient times!

Lucretia

This legendary heroine played a key role in the creation of the Roman Republic. As a noblewoman and virtuous wife to the cruel Lucius Tarquinius Collatinus, she symbolized both purity and beauty, making her the 'ideal' Roman lady. After her tragic death, her story of challenging her husband's authority inspired the overthrow of the monarchy. This led to the formation of the Roman Republic – it was their first democracy (which meant citizens had a right to vote on laws) and this marked a turning point in Roman history.

Claudia Quinta

This heroine's most important job was to keep the sacred fire, which the Romans believed had been brought from Troy to Rome by Aeneas, burning forever. When she was falsely accused of breaking her vow, her life was in mortal danger, but with the help of the goddess Cybele, an ancient mother goddess from the East, Claudia Quinta proved her innocence by rescuing a sunken ship from the River Tiber. Her bravery not only saved her life, but also showed young Roman girls how powerful and important women could be in Roman society!

CAMILLA

Camilla was a legendary fierce warrior and queen of the Volscians, blessed by the goddess Diana. She was so speedy she could run across the sea without making a single ripple and fought bravely alongside the Roman king Turnus against Aeneas. Although she lost her life in battle, Camilla challenged gender roles and inspired both strength and courage in a society that was ruled by men!

HERCULES

Hercules, the mighty demigod and son of Jupiter, was a hero loved by both the Greeks and Romans. As a baby, he was hunted by the vengeful goddess Juno (Jupiter's wife), but his incredible strength saved him from a snake she sent to destroy him, and later, he became a champion of the weak by completing twelve seemingly impossible labours (missions). One of these labours included slaying the huge Nemean lion and he wore the lion's golden fur as a trophy. But despite his strength, Hercules could still feel pain, suffer injuries and get tired – just like you and me!

AENEAS

Aeneas, the son of Venus (goddess of love and beauty), was a brave hero who fought alongside his cousin Hector to defend the city of Troy from the Greeks. After the city was destroyed, he led the remaining Trojans to Italy, where they founded the city of Lavinium, near Rome. Aeneas became a symbol of Roman values like bravery, loyalty and devotion, helping to shape the future of Roman civilization.

Romulus and Remus

Romulus and Remus, the legendary twin brothers born to a human mother and the god of war, Mars, were left on the banks of the River Tiber. They were found by a she-wolf who nursed them until they were rescued by a shepherd. As adults, the twins overthrew the evil king who had wanted them dead and decided to build a city along the River Tiber: Rome. In a fierce argument, Romulus took the life of Remus and went on to found Rome, becoming its first king and giving the Romans a legendary origin that linked them to the gods and their divine power!

Numa Pompilius

Numa Pompilius, the second king of Rome, is remembered as a wise and devoted ruler who laid the foundations of Roman religion by establishing new cults, such as the cults of Mars, Jupiter and Romulus. Guided and favoured by a nymph (a female spirit) called Egeria, he chose priests and priestesses to serve the gods, strengthening Rome's protection through religious practices. Although not an adventurous hero, Numa taught the Romans to follow the law, show respect to enemies and live wisely. He also reformed the calendar, adding the months of January and February, which we still use today!

Gaius Mucius Scaevola

Gaius Mucius Scaevola became famous for his fearless defiance of an Etruscan king who had captured Rome. To prove his bravery, Gaius Mucius Scaevola placed his hand in a fire without showing that he was experiencing any pain (you MUST NOT try this at home!), shocking the enemy and earning his safe return to Rome. His 'courageous' act (again, you MUST NOT try this at home – if you put your hand in fire, you'll end up being horribly burnt) not only shocked the Etruscan king but also helped secure a peace agreement, preventing a war and showing the Roman values of bravery and determination!

Empresses and Emperors

Fulvia Flacca Bambula – Influential c. 52–40 BCE

Although never actually an empress, as the third wife to the general Mark Antony, Fulvia was a daring woman with real influence, challenging Octavian's rise to power (among others). She was also known as 'Queen of the Roman Street Gangs', because she encouraged everyday working people and angry mobs (who were loyal to her) to rise up against her rivals. Fulvia was a woman not to be messed with!

Livia Drusilla – Empress 27 BCE–14 CE

Livia Drusilla was an intelligent, powerful wife to Emperor Augustus. As his personal advisor, Livia helped run important parts of Rome's growing trade, such as copper mines and papyrus marshes. Her wisdom proved very useful in politics, making her a key figure in the empire. People across Rome's territories admired her so much that coins, statues, races and even oaths were produced in her honour!

Agrippina the Younger – Empress 49–54 CE

Agrippina, one of the most famous empresses of the Julio-Claudian dynasty, was considered so noble and influential that her face appeared on coins next to her son, Emperor Nero – this was unheard of at the time! She earned the title Securitas, symbolizing both the strength and safety of the Roman Empire through her relationships with the Senate and her powerful marriages. Admired and envied by many, Agrippina was both a respected and feared figure in Roman history.

Julia Domna – Empress 193–211 CE

Julia Domna was born in Syria, and before her marriage to Emperor Septimius Severus, an astrologer predicted she would marry a king. She would later receive the important titles of Augusta (Sacred Female Founder), Mater Augustus (Mother of Augustus) and Mater Castrorum (Mother of the Camp). Accompanying Severus on campaigns, she brought wealth and prosperity to the city of Eboracum (York). She remains one of the only empresses to hold a number of official titles. Many Romans cherished her opinions as she supported artists, thinkers and scholars, creating an

influential circle devoted to the progress of philosophy. Most famous of these was a man called Philostratus, who wrote *Life of Apollonius of Tyana* – a very popular book in the Roman Empire. One day you should read it!

Ulpia Severina – Empress 270–275 CE

Bestowed with the title of Augusta, Domina Ulpia Severina Augusta, as both empress and politician, championed the influence and presence of women in Roman politics. The only empress to rule without an emperor, her image was minted into coins, which spread around Rome's empire, building her wealth, influence and power.

Gaius Julius Caesar Augustus (Augustus Octavian) – Ruled 27 BCE–14 CE

Gaius Julius Caesar Augustus, great-nephew and adopted son of Julius Caesar, became Rome's first emperor after defeating Mark Antony and Cleopatra VII in a civil war. Later known as Augustus Octavian, he expanded the Roman Empire to twice its size, encouraging 200 years of 'peace' called the Pax Romana. Augustus built grand temples, introduced a postal system and constructed roads, leading to the expression 'all roads lead to Rome!'

Gaius Caesar (Caligula) – Ruled 37–41 CE

Caligula, known as the 'mad' emperor, got his nickname, meaning 'little soldier boot', from wearing miniature armour as a child while following his war hero father, Germanicus. He was a wild ruler, but he also did lots of good, such as building theatres, temples and aqueducts to bring water, and (less of a good idea) thrilling the people with gladiatorial games. But after an accident, Caligula's behaviour became very bizarre – he tried to give his horse a role in the Senate, he forced all the people of Rome to worship him as a god, and he even declared war on the god of the sea, Neptune!

Nero Claudius Caesar Augustus Germanicus – Ruled 54–68 CE

At just sixteen years old, Nero became emperor, and while rumour says he burned Rome to the ground, his reign was both terrifying and full of twists and turns. Nero made it possible for slaves to take cruel masters to court. He also widened roads, stopped some gladiator killings and even enforced rules for safer buildings made of brick or stone. But Nero wasn't great with family – he ordered for the murder of his mother, as well as two wives and many rivals! Through his tyranny he became lazy and careless, leading the Senate to declare him an enemy of Rome in 68 CE.

HADRIAN – RULED 117–138 CE

Hadrian, the first of Rome's 'Five Good Emperors', and nicknamed the 'Greekling', was the first emperor to have a full beard, heavily inspired by Greek culture. Hadrian journeyed across the Mediterranean and beyond, ensuring peace and security for the empire by creating laws that protected all Roman citizens (even some slaves too), while building remarkable structures like Hadrian's Wall in northern England. Hadrian also helped rebuild and establish new temples in Egypt, Rome and Greece, all the while encouraging the enjoyment of arts and literature.

MARCUS AURELIUS – RULED 161–180 CE

Marcus, known as '*Verissimus*' (meaning 'the truest one'), was a Stoic philosopher and emperor who mastered Greek and Latin, and wrote the book *Meditations* between 171 and 175 CE. As the last of the Five Good Emperors, his reign was marked by wealth and a love for humour, as he believed that comedy and sports improved people's lives. He also held a deep respect for ancient law and the Senate. Under his leadership the Roman Empire enjoyed a golden age, inspiring many – even today – to live a good and honest life.

ACKNOWLEDGEMENTS

It is brilliant to be surrounded by people who love what they do. This book would not have been possible without the help of Tabitha Chamberlayne, Chloe Wheeler and Celia Riddiough. And none of it would even have happened had it not been for the inspiration of my fabulous teachers Veronica Anstey and Mary Sergeant and dear departed Miss Cawthorne – I thank you, and I thank all the teachers there ever have been and ever will be. Well done, Arlo, Evie, Nell, Janie and her brilliant Class 30 for reading the first draft of this book and coming back with such excellent ideas. Thank you to Nathan for the absolutely fantastic illustrations! Phoebe, thank you too for being unbelievably patient waiting for the raw material . . . which was often delayed by me trying to write it on storm-tossed high seas, or in caves in the desert, or from Roman burial sites halfway up mountains. But the thing is, the Romans spread so far, they had their fingers in so many pies and they got into so many nooks and crannies of the world, I had to try really hard to get to the bottom of their incredible story. This meant I've had to be away a lot, so this book is also for my own two girls, who are divine. I'm looking forward to many more adventures and journeys through time and across space with them.